FROM TOULOUSE-LAUTREC TO RODIN

Arthur Symons

FROM
TOULOUSE-LAUTREC
TO RODIN

WITH SOME PERSONAL IMPRESSIONS

by

ARTHUR SYMONS

Essay Index Reprint Series

BOOKS FOR LIBRARIES PRESS

FREEPORT, NEW YORK

First Published 1930
Reprinted 1968

LIBRARY OF CONGRESS CATALOG CARD NUMBER:
68-20342

CONTENTS

v

LIST OF ILLUSTRATIONS

FROM TOULOUSE-LAUTREC TO RODIN

FROM TOULOUSE-LAUTREC TO RODIN

HENRI DE TOULOUSE-LAUTREC

I

LAUTREC has his place, in which he is unique, among the painters of our century who have deliberately turned backward or aside ; some haters of their own time, some haters of reality : such as Gustave Moreau, Puvis de Chavannes, Simeon Solomon, Burne-Jones, Felicien Rops and Aubrey Beardsley. Most of them are not perfectly equipped as painters—Beardsley being otherwise equipped than a painter ; but they may seem to escape from some at least of their limitations by this commerce with another world. All have an interest beyond their mere skill as painters, with various kinds of appeal to those who go to art for something which is certainly not the art of it. Some have a devil—others speak with tongues. They set up wayside idols to strange gods, and bow down before the Prince of the Powers of the Air.

Lautrec burns always with an inordinate desire of women, an inveterate desire ; and, being immensely rich, he has also *un mépris de la vie et une haine exaspérée contre la femme en général*. This phrase simply means the same thing as Baudelaire's cynical contempt for women ; but, in both cases, the phrase is a paradox. Whenever he dined, for instance, in *Le Rat Mort*, he would call to a woman he admired : "*Arrêtez-vous !*" and he would take out his notebook and draw some passionate design of her ; then he would get up and wander round the tables, drinking in women's beauty as if he literally drank—as vampires do—their flesh and blood.

His exasperating sense of contrasting colours is one of the qualities of his *macabre* genius. Nothing revolts him ; he paints beauty and ugliness, with a superb indifference ; he paints vice and ignoble and exotic and atrocious and obscene creatures with the absolute insolence, the utter cynicism of some Satan or of some God who created in mutual antagonism the cruel and adorable world we live in.

In some of his pictures I see transmutations of venomous and viperine beings, coloured with pernicious pigments into symbolical creations and into shadows and into dire mysteries ; the deification of the absolute Evil, the diabolism of the absolute Good ; the alchemist before his crucibles, who bends over his lighted fire ; the Impure Poet who has read his Baudelaire.; the Painter who has learnt from Manet and from Degas : who yet remains insolently original.

With a god's gaiety and a devil's merriment he jests with his tools—but all his jests have in them an intense and an enraged bitterness. Day and night, night and day, continues this ruinous existence of his ; often exhausted with sleepless nights, always over-nervous, over-sensitive, over-excitable ; an existence of so intolerable a nature that even he himself never wholly divines the dangers that lie in his way. Peril means to him a mere mockery. And it is impossible to say how evil Lautrec was and how much evil contagion he spread around him.

Such genius as his proves at times suicidal; he certainly had no intention of ruining his life, but the evil powers within him contending with the few virtues he possessed, the enormity and the prodigality of his passions, brought down too soon the house of life over his head.

He had a devil in him; that devil set his imagination spinning webs that were not webs, set him to distort image after image, which he never could help either disturbing or deforming or distorting; for he was *homo duplex*; and this double nature never left him alone, never gave him enough rest. It is said he had a lovable nature; nor can I, who have known him, deny this fact. But, as the word meant at times so much to him, and more often less than nothing, he usually dispensed with the word; nor need I substitute the word he named in its place. Having only one vice, the vice for women, he was not entirely abnormal; yet the man himself was so much a mixture of the human and the inhuman that I never knew when he passed from one stage to another. And with all his fascinating perversity, his hatred of mediocrity, his terror of death, Lautrec was—essentially—a Painter, and therein lay the superstructure of normality without which there can be no creation.

He had stormy blood—or the menacing blood of what was so ancient in his race—and he had a splendid intelligence and an imagination always at work, and, in his veins, impure fires. " He was neither God nor madman nor man to be adored." I quote Meredith. Lautrec was adored, thought by some to be a fool,

3

and by many to be a madman ; he was, in certain senses, a Tragic Comedian. He saw, to his cost, the comic and tragic sides of life ; and his death was tragic, he died tragically young, at the age of thirty-seven.

Indeed, how can such a life as Lautrec's—lived, as it were, from instant to instant, at almost actually the same speed as Rossetti's, of whom Pater said, " His life was a crisis at every moment " ; when the life of the imagination is always in conflict with the life of the senses, when the inner world only brings disquieting tidings from the outer world ; when one's life-blood wars with one's veritable life—be conceived as anything less fatal than by stating the fact that the flame in his blood fed on flames ? In depraved vision he leans over the abyss of hell and gazes unperturbed on the agonies of the damned. Perturbed he indicates the insane desires of woman for man, of human reptile for human reptile, the murderous divisions of the sexes ; the perdition that waits for all—one imagines —that have sinned in vain and in vain repented ; the hell beyond all one's desire, the heaven beyond the seven circles of the hells. Yet these degraded beings, who endure callously enough their degradation, are not created by a man who hates them ; he paints them as they are and not as they are. Their eyes and mouths thirst for they know not what ; they have no other sense but that of flesh for flesh. They stand as he makes them stand—stupid beyond stupidity, beautiful, perverse, inhuman ; he sets them in motion when he chooses to, and we see the skirts of the dancing women in the air, and the slower rhythms of their dances. And for some sinister reason—I never was certain if he altogether knew it himself—there is almost always (there are rare and wonderful exceptions) something ignoble, sullen, torpid, turbulent, vehement, excitable and unimpulsive in these creatures who exist ; one knows, certainly, where they exist : in evil houses, in the streets, in the balls, in the café-concerts, in the music-halls ; and that they are always astonishingly alive.

We see them live, drink, talk, dance, gesticulate ; they sit at tables—as in Degas's paintings—leaning over half-empty bottles of wine, as in the case of a depraved girl, dazed with the wine she has drunk, her eyes fixed on nothing, only they seem to be occupied with unreal dreams ; her nose is ugly, her mouth thick, her hair bedraggled ; she leans with both elbows on the table, with her right hand clenched on her throat, the left supporting her chin ; she wears a white blouse, and she is alone. And to me his vision of her is so intense that what is sordid in her becomes tragic ; he even makes me pity her—he has made her so human, and yet, so lost a woman.

I I

PART of the technique of Lautrec consists, not only in his original way of seeing, but in his seeing things, not in subdivisions, nor in shades, but in masses, each single ; so that when he sabres some form of infamous flesh with peroxide of hydrogen colour—when he paints green where there is no green ; when he uses an aniline dye, that poisons nature ; when he casts green shadows on faces and gets some particular tinge of green into his flesh colours, and more curious tinges of green mixed with the red of rouge on women's

B

painted faces—it seems as if this morbid painter were anticipating the colour schemes of the grave.

I have said before, " Lautrec has a devil in him." I think that, when the Devil entered into him, his temptations were seven : yet out of the seven colours Lautrec used, those he preferred were all kinds of greens, many different shades of yellow and fiery reds. He had a passion for brutal colours, in violent, and often excessive contrasts ; yet, having no passion for perfection, he masses his colours as he masses his creations, with an absolute mastery of his material ; and composes his picture in a way so entirely his own, that these amazingly living, hideous, revolting Parisians are turned into consummate images, images not even symbolical, but that have for me an inevitable fascination. Take *L'Assommoir*. It is suggested by Zola's novel ; I find in it merely a suggestion, and—think but for the moment of the question of Art—the difference between the man of talent and the man of genius is immense. And it is here I would complain, not as a matter of morals, but as a matter of art, of Zola's obsession by what is grossly, uninterestingly filthy. There is a certain simile in the novel I have referred to used in the most innocent connection, in connection with a bonnet, which seems to me the most abjectly dirty phrase which I have ever read. Now I will not say, think of all Lautrec's paintings, but think of them on the whole, and I would challenge any reasonable critic to point out where their indecency exists ; and I would answer : Neither more nor less than in Cassanova than in Aristophanes, than in Rabelais, than in certain things in the Bible.

In *A la Mie* the situation is wholly changed. A

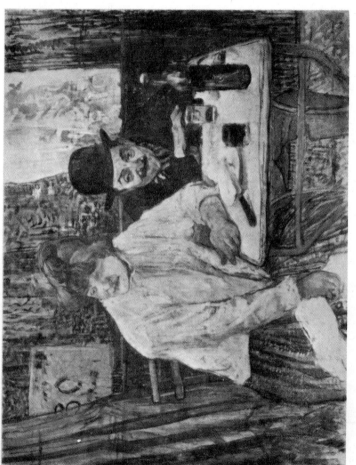

TOULOUSE-LAUTREC

A La Mie

woman dressed like the other one, but with a savage and attractive face, shown clearly under her mass of hair, turns away—and in how natural a moment of spite—from a hideous man, a man absolutely vile, a criminal, lower perhaps than a criminal, who, with hat on head and arms crossed on the table, grimaces at I know not what night shadow. The situation is what I have always seen in Paris; only changed by Lautrec's genius into what I can only call *Un Conte Cruel*, and one that Villiers might have liked to have written.

I have said somewhere that Lautrec juggles with iron bars and masses of shadow; only, as a rule, these masses are cut off in angles on both sides of a picture: a manner of painting which he certainly caught from Degas. In one of his finest creations, *Le Clown*, the woman herself is superb in madness, glory, stupor, lust; she is painted in macabre colours—a genius in gestures. There is in the conception a taint of corruption; she has a dead splendour of *mat couleur*: she has red hair and her dress is spotted with colours of orange and of blood. *La Danseuse* has stupor and a licentious gaze, the red mouth wide open, the breasts shown; her arms are thin, her fingers clasped; she has meagre legs and pink raw tights, an ample white skirt painted with a bizarre blue. There are reds and yellows in the colour scheme. There lives she, yawns; she is exasperatingly young, corrupt in flesh—an uncouth ugliness in the face. *La femme à mi-corps* has a face of rare beauty—a face Augustus John might have painted—with her coiled black hair and voluptuous mouth and wicked eyes; she is painted with violent red and blue and yellow colours. She is not even a Flower of Evil.

7

Always Lautrec fixes in music-halls the absolute
certainty of every gesture, of every livid line of the
painted faces, of every awkward movement; the
grimaces of lips and cheeks—the light cast on these
singers from the footlights. You hear the music and
you see the dancing, and you feel the music's rhythm
and the dancer's cadences. Lautrec can be as lyrical
and literally erotic as Aristophanes, to whose genius
I have referred, for he combines in an extraordinary
fashion the complexities of modern life as they turn
from comedy to tragedy, and then return into their
elemental clay. All are jaded, all are Parisian, many
of them are not intrinsically interesting, only Lautrec
gives them certain subtleties of his own—he insists
on their interesting us. And, in his limited range of
characters, many are as various as life itself; however
trivial, or unlovely, or misshapen, they come under his
magic. And in Lautrec's world there are no laws, no
rules, no morals, no beliefs, no negations; no acceptance of anything but of the fact of having suddenly
been awakened into life, to await, in these latter days,
God's judgment. And, in all this, Lautrec's pride
is so illimitable that he gives to none of his creatures
any of his pride.

Something of the rage in his blood causes at times a
disturbance in the very mediums and values he paints
with. And it is his jarred nerves that account for
much of the dissonances and discords in his particular
gamut of colours; for in his painting, as in all painting,
a sense of music is allied with a sense of colour. Walter
Pater in his essay on *The School of Giorgione*, in which
he came perhaps nearer to a complete or final dis-
entangling of the meanings and functions of the arts

8

than any writer on æsthetics has yet done, tells us :
All art constantly aspires towards the condition of music.
And of music because, " in its ideal, consummate
moments, the end is not distinct from the means, the
form from the matter, the subject from the expression ;
and to it, therefore, to the condition of its perfect
moments, all the arts may be supposed constantly to
tend and aspire."

Art has little to do with the brain apart from the
emotions ; the brain, apart from the emotions, pro-
duces in art only the artificial or the fantastic. These
latter qualities are by no means absent from Lautrec's
work ; but emotion in him is strangely evident in those
creations of his who seem always to be struggling in
vain to produce emotional states. And they are for
the most part created out of Lautrec's disturbed nerves,
for are not the disturbance of their nerves written all
over them ?

French painters, as I have pointed out elsewhere,
from Courbet to Degas, have come to believe not that
beauty can only be rendered by fine technique, but
that beauty can be found in technique only. Degas
is typical of that school to which subject-matter is
indifferent, treatment everything. Or it would be
more correct to say that the uglier the subject the
better excuse does it give for virtuosity of technique,
so that Degas, in his revolt against the academic treatment of the nude, has a way of stripping a woman-
model, setting her to stand in a tin bath and squeeze
a sponge over her shoulders, so that the attitude reveals
every physical degradation of age, the very impress
of the whalebones of the corset ; so, under very
different conditions does at times Lautrec, but with

9

much less virtuosity. But, where Lautrec never dares to compete with Degas, is when Degas paints, behind the scenes, two homely girls in practising dress, straining a leg forward and backward, while the shoulder-blades stand out like knives, and the whole body aches with effort.

There are times when Lautrec's vision is that of a creature of jarred nerves, who shudders at the contact of the crowd, and averts his eyes from the ugliness of suffering and the soil of labour ; and is rarely happy under the grossness of sunlight—and yet the sunlight means so much to him, this painter—for his joy, and a joy of all the senses is when night comes on and the lamps are lighted and the red wings of the Moulin-Rouge turn, turn under ghosts of sunset.

I have said of Monticelli that he painted colour as a musician might be content to weave dissonances into fantastic progressions, in a kind of very conscious madness, a Sadism of sound. This cannot be said of Lautrec's paintings, except in the violence of his vision when sounds intoxicate him, and he gives us back the abstract intoxication of the eyes—indicated in terms of cruelty and lust, that torture us with their strange abnormal beauty ; as if one's sensuality cried out as the colours cry at us with the pain of an ecstasy that we cannot bear.

Lautrec has many of the evil qualities of Beardsley, whose drawings he certainly admired ; and of whom I have said, " He found, in the French art of the moment, a joyous sadness, the service to God of Mephistopheles which his own temperament and circumstances were waiting to suggest to him." To Beardsley sin meant everything; to Lautrec sin was simply a matter of the flesh. His people, the greater part of them, have sinful faces, and he is certainly unconcerned with the souls that struggle under the skin. And to him evil never purifies itself ; yet he is always vividly awake to evil. And, what meaning could Lautrec have attached to Gautier's famous paradox, that " perfection of line is virtue " ? None ; for to him deformity was his genius. And, when all is said, only three modern painters could have achieved so simple a masterpiece as that of painting a man sitting at a café table and drinking absinthe : Manet, Degas, Lautrec.

III

WRITING elsewhere on Montmartre and La Butte, and referring to what one saw there in the way of Bruant's heroes and heroines, the lady on her way to Saint-Lazare, the gentleman—who knows ?—perhaps to La Roquette, who rested from their (as one names it) labours and who, leaning over the wooden paling as I used to, year after year, including the present year, enjoying Paris impressionistically ; it occurred to me then, as it does now, that this is one of the gifts of the *esprit Montmartre*, that philosophy of the pavement which has always been localized in this district. And, exactly as I found them in other years, so this year at Montmartre—and here essentially—are almost all the public balls, the really Parisian café-concerts, which exist in Paris. And that is why amusing Paris used to, but no longer does—amusing Paris, as it then was—go to Montmartre.

I give two visions of Montmartre, written in dif-

II

ferent years, and from a different point of view. In
no other city can I recall anything in itself so sordidly
picturesque as these crawling heights, which lead up
to the Butte, so wonderful as the vision of the city
which the Butte gives one. I know Montmartre chiefly
by night. When you have climbed as high as you
can climb, ending almost with ladders, you reach a
dreary little strip of ground, on which a wooden paling seems to hold you back from falling sheer into
the abyss of Paris. Under a wild sky the city floats
away endlessly, a vague, immense vision of forests of
houses, softened by fringes of actual forest ; but for
the most part it is but a succession of light and shade,
here tall white houses coming up out of a pit of
shadows, there an unintelligible mass of darkness,
sheered through by an inexplicable arrow of light.
Right down below one looks straight into the lighted
windows, distinguishing the figure which moves about
the room ; while, in the far distance, there is nothing
but a faint reddish haze, rising dubiously into the
night, as if the lusts of Paris smoked to the skies.
Night after night I have been up to this odd, fascinating little corner, mainly to look at all I had left
behind.

It is June, 1920, and I have found my way up the
steep, curious, thronged and narrow rue Lepic, that
leads to the Moulin de la Galette, and, after climbing
ladder after ladder, I find myself on the Butte. The
vision I have of Paris is of something unending,
immense, unreal yet real under a misty sky where the
horizon ends in smoke. I see Notre Dame, formidable, roofs and roofs and roofs, domes and chimneys,
houses tightly packed together in an intolerable man-

ner. Below me streets, and no people, except in one ; on all sides below me are open windows and balconies and wretched flower-pots, and faces and faces, and rags—almost Venetian rags—and then space. There is a kind of naked sublimity as I gaze from this height on Paris : stupendous, a *Méryon*, a mass of surging demons, of evil spirits.

One afternoon in May I found myself on the Place Blanche, Boulevard de Clichy, Montmartre. I went there deliberately with the intention of discovering what might remain of the Moulin-Rouge I had haunted year after year, summer and spring and winter. Then I used to meet, not only Toulouse-Lautrec, either alone or seated with *chahut* dancers at the little tables on both sides of the hall ; but the greater part of these extraordinary women, from Nini-Patte-en-l'Air, the oldest and most learned of them, whose roving eyes had a curious and intent glitter, who I named " the Mænad of the Decadence," to the *gamine* who was then La Goulue, and who was supposed, wrongly, to have genius ; and from these to Grille-d'Égout, who deserved her nickname ; and from her—apart from La Sauterelle, Étoile Filante, La Macarona—who had an extraordinary effrontery—Églantine, Épi-d'Or, La Ténébreuse (who was tenebrous) ; from these to the adorable, the fascinating beyond all imaginable fascination, La Mélinite, whose name in the world was Jane Avril.

On that afternoon I had gone in a taxi from La Place de la Concorde to la rue Pigalle, and had climbed up that steep street. *Dans les temps de jadis* I generally went from the Latin Quarter on that ponderous omnibus, the " Batignolle-Clichy-Odéon," right across

Paris, across streets I know by heart—such as the ambiguous Chaussée-d'Antin—and then up the rue Notre Dame-de-Lorette, which, however much favoured by the Lorettes of the time of Gavarni, may still be, perhaps, less favoured by their unillustrious descendants of the rue de Bréda and other similar streets, to the point where I got out ; to see before me, as if at the other side of the street, across the broad open space of the Place Blanche, the red bulk and waving sails of the Moulin-Rouge.

I am as avid of discoveries as of adventures : I have had far and away too many adventures, in unequal mixtures of good and bad ones, for the most infallible memory to remember ; I have made certain original discoveries, all of which have gone into my books ; as for this last adventure, which I supposed could be nothing less than a misadventure, it turned out to be —certainly—sinister. I saw—I saw to my surprise— on the opposite side of the square, the black and rusty red ruins of the Moulin-Rouge ; the huge wheels that used to turn, turn, always under glowing sunsets, stained by the sunset's fiery colour, were black, hideously black, and ominously silent. The crescent at the top had faded as the faintest crescent moon fades into the night ; an ironical image, it seemed to me, of what is the ruling star of the Turks, seen on every height in Constantinople. I went across to gaze up to these ruins—ruins left to themselves, as such ruins ought to be, in Paris—from the *Cabaret le Grelot* ; even the name of the Moulin-Rouge is not effaced. One ought always to respect—as Parisians mostly do— names that remain, in one's memory, wonderful. Over one of the doors, under a grimacing girl's image

14

above it, I read : " Quadrilles. Dimanches et Fêtes. Matinées à trois heures. Bal à Orchestre." Then— sadly or not—I went my way in another direction.

Montmartre was in Lautrec's blood ; Montmartre possessed him, as it were bodily and unspiritually. The Moulin-Rouge was certainly glorious to Henri de Toulouse-Lautrec ; he made it more glorious than it ever was. Once inside he sought for the physical signs of the vices of men and of women. The red wings of the Windmill turned, turned, flower-like, every night ; it was always to me a matter of intense excitement— for I never knew what surprises, what chances, what hazards might not meet me at any given moment ; a dancing-girl, a street girl, a Lesbian. So these Parisian and decadent enchantments seized furiously on this painter's heart—on so much of his life, on so much of his genius.

IV

To be great, to be a man of genius, to be famous, to be much loved and much hated, to be much praised and much dispraised ; to have a passion for creation and a passion for women ; to be descended from one of the oldest French families ; to be abnormal and inhuman ; to be neither dissipated nor degenerate ; to have sardonic humour and intense presence of mind ; to adore nights more than days—to adore and to detest immensely ; to squander much of one's substance in riotous living, to have a terribly direct eye and as direct a force of hand ; to be capable of painting certain things which have never yet existed for us on the canvas ; to be angry with his material, as his brutal instincts seize hold on him ; these, chosen at random, are certain of the distinguishing qualities of Lautrec—certain of his elemental emotions.

I am inclined to apply to Lautrec this sentence I wrote in Naples on Saint Augustine : " Intellectual pride, one sees in him indeed at all times, by the very force with which it is repressed into humility ; and, in all that relates to that mistress, in the famous cry, ' Give me chastity, but not yet ! ' we see the force of the flesh, in one who lived always with so passionate a life, alike of the spirit and of the senses." This lyrical cry Lautrec might have uttered in a moment of sensual rapture ; for, as we all sin, so we exult over our sins in a most vivid remembrance of them ; with, rarely, the vision of chastity wavering on our restless imaginations. It is with the same lyrical rage that Castiza, in *The Revenger's Tragedy*, hurls at her unchaste mother these words :

> Mother, come from that poisonous woman there !

So, with all a lover's passionate hate, Catullus cries at Lesbia :

> Ah ! This torpor that creeps like a poison from vein to vein,
> Every joy that was once a joy from my heart has chased :
> Now I ask no longer that she should love me again,
> Or, what never can be, that she would choose to be chaste.

Yet, to return to Toulouse-Lautrec, who was himself the ultimate of his curiosities, was it himself, really, that he had been seeking all the time, conscious at least of that in all the deviations of his way ?

Lautrec had a collection of curious idols ; and some might have resembled those of Hippolytus. " Very different, certainly, from the cruel-featured little idol his mother had brought in her bundle—the old

Scythian Artemis, hanging on the wall, side by side
with the forgotten Ceres, blood-red, reveals herself as
a virgin." "You could hardly tell," I continue to
quote Pater, "where the apartment of the adulteress
ended and that of the divine courtesan began. Haunts
of her long, indolent, self-pleasing nights and days,
they represented everywhere the impress of Phædra's
luxurious humour." How such luxurious sensations
as these would have appealed to Lautrec's luxurious
taste ; might indeed have inspired him to create a
picture representing the courtesan's room, with the
cruel idols on the walls, the glow of heady lamplight,
the scent of the incense, the dizzy wheel that turns, as
Phædra cuts secretly from her son shreds of stuff
from his sleeve—and, crouching as in some unclean
sty or shrine the almost formless goddess, clad afresh
in piquant change of raiment.

Lautrec never saw "life in the round," as Balzac
did, immensely ; he had none of Balzac's creative
genius, in spite of the originality of his own genius ;
and yet, as I read this sentence I wrote on Balzac in
Madrid : " For Balzac is the equivalent of great cities,"
some of what is most elemental in Lautrec's work—
which is entirely and absolutely Parisian—seems to
be summed up in this phrase ; only, for " great cities "
read " Paris." I can but conjecture that the love of
Balzac for Paris was as passionate as Lautrec's ; conjectures are vain ; but the truth is that, as there is
abnormality in the genius of these two artists, certainly
they had a passion for the abnormal. Take, for
instance, *La Fille aux Yeux d'or, Sarrasine,* certain
pages of *Père Goriot.* The abnormality of Goriot is
that his unjustified passion for his faithless daughters

is as abnormal as King Lear's. Goriot is a Lear at heart, and he suffers the same tortures and humiliations. But where Lear grows up before the mind's eye into a vast cloud and shadowy monument of trouble, Goriot grows downward into the earth and takes root there, wrapping the dust about all his fibres.

Take *Une Passion dans le Désert* (1830), and read it as I read it in *La Revue de Paris* ; and, having finished it, try to imagine how much of this passion of the panther for the man is normal and how much is abnormal.

" La Tête se distinguait par une rare expression de finesse, la froide cruauté des tigres y dominait bien, mais il y avait aussi une vague ressemblance avec le physionomie d'une femme artificieuse. Enfin la figure de cette reine solitaire révélait en ce moment une sorte de gaieté semblable à celle de Néron ivre : elle s'était désalterée dans le sang et voulait jouir."

Compare with this *La Belle Impéria* and almost the whole of *Les Contes Drôlatiques*, and again I can but imagine that the preponderance is in favour of abnormality.

V

WHEN I read, in *Le Figaro*, that there was some fantastic idea in the vivid imagination of the Parisians of rebuilding the Moulin-Rouge, it seemed to me that one might as well conceive the idea of rebuilding the Tower of Babel, where a thousand tongues spoke in a thousand languages. That is what I said to myself, before I went to Paris, in 1924. No sooner had I arrived there, and settled down in a hotel in the Latin Quarter, than I determined to make certain discoveries, in regard to Lautrec and the Moulin-Rouge. It was on June 7th that I explored Montmartre, from nine in the morning till midnight. What I really wanted to find was his studio in la rue Tourlaque, which he left in January, 1899, for another, in la rue Frochot, which gives on la rue Bréda. I came on it on my way to the Moulin de la Galette ; it is on the right of the steep and turning rue Lépic, which crosses la rue Thelozé, then turns sideways into a steeper street that leads to the long dreary rue Domrémy.

I saw the big studio in which he used to paint, on the top floor of No. 5, at the corner of these two streets. As I stood there, gazing up with a kind of reverence, a lovely borzois came up and caressed me, gently, deliciously. Up came after him the strange little harlot to whom the borzois belonged, bag in hand. She said to me : " *Hé bien ! Le patron ! Comment ça va ?* " We fell into conversation ; she was amusing, she had a passion for her lovely beast. Finally, after some persuasion on her part, both of them went into the door of No. 5. She was an amazing being to have met just then ; by some mere accident, some luck, some fortune such as often falls to me. She was an absolute Lautrec—*sur le vif.* She was small, perverse, with very wicked eyes ; and, apart from her evident sordidness, she was not without that charm which such women are capable of showing.

After I left her, I was determined, if possible, to enter the Moulin-Rouge, and my desire was gratified. They had begun repairs. I went into a chaos of dust and lumber, of untidiness and of disorder ; of confusion and of a kind of annihilation. There, as always, painted plain, was " Consommations Obligatoires."

The more I penetrated into the interior the more I felt that I was entering an obscure night. The more I penetrated into this obscure night the more the vision returned to me of Seville and of my purchase in les Sierpes of the rare first edition of *Obras Espirituales*, 1618, of San Juan de la Cruz; and of that strange, fantastic figure which stands at the beginning of the *Salida del Monte Carmelo*, and the narrow way which leads to the mount which is inscribed " Nothing." The sensation I had when I read this book in Seville, as obscure as that night which is the negation of all things, was almost identical with the one I experienced in the obscurity of the Moulin-Rouge. Again the aspect of Chaos, an extraordinary effect; low entrances, dark and dreary; tables heaped on one another as they used to be: in a word, the Dust of Ages! An almost hideous accumulation of dust almost suffocated me. On one yellow door I read: *Poussez*. The colours were yellower than ever. I saw the two ways by which we used to go into the Ball— the two separate doors. I saw vaguely chairs on the tops of tables, tables on the tops of chairs, all sorts of iron things and wooden things, and, very conspicuously, two tattered wooden representations of the flames of hell (as I imagined), the red paint much worn from their artichoke-like shoots. Almost as sinister was the man who had the keys of the Moulin-Rouge: the typical *gueux* of Montmartre.

VI

THE Moulin-Rouge was certainly glorious to Henri de Toulouse-Lautrec; he made it more glorious than it ever was. Once inside, he sought for the physical signs of the vices of men and of women. The red wings of the Windmill turned, flame-like, every night; always to me a matter of intense excitement. So these Parisian and decadent enchantments seized furiously on this painter's heart ; on, also, much of his life, on much of his genius.

In the Moulin-Rouge, night after night, a special table was always reserved for Lautrec. He sat there for hours, showing, as he did elsewhere, that nervous exasperation which rarely left him. In the intervals of their dances, the *chahut* dancers crowded around him ; often he would make them sit down and give them drinks and then draw them. After that he would get up, feverishly, take a few turns in the hall. So, as he was the only painter who absolutely adored it, in his pictures of this night-haunt and of other night-haunts of an equally evil character, he created stupendous effects, which I can only compare with those of Degas : in both an equal nobility, an equal comprehension, of these enigmatical creatures ; of the inexorable stains and configurations of sin.

A *bastringue* the Moulin-Rouge certainly was, and, in its way, unsurpassable ; equally in the curious fascination with which I always entered it and in the fascination of the *chahut* dancers. The three who were most famous for their extraordinary talents were La Mélinite, La Goulue and Valentin the disjointed ; who certainly deserved his name, for he danced with an amazing dexterity, his thin legs defied caricature ; and he, like the others, rarely lost his rhythm.

La Goulue was a strange and tall girl, with a vampire's face, the profile of a bird of prey, a tortured mouth, and metallic eyes ; who danced always with definite gestures ; I heard all kinds of legends in regard to her life ; death and sensuality and blood ; which is my version of the title of one of Barrès' books ; who certainly joined with the avid circle that tightened round the quadrille dancers. Once the music started, up went the skirts and the heels to the level of their faces.

I first met La Mélinite on an unforgettable night in May, 1892, at Le Jardin de Paris. She danced in a Quadrille : young and girlish, the more provocative because she played as a prude, with an assumed modesty, *décolletée* nearly to her waist, in the Oriental fashion. She had long black curls around her face ; and had about her an air of depraved virginity.

She told me she was dancing the next night at the Moulin-Rouge, and asked me to meet her there, which I certainly did. I give here, word for word, the notes I made that night—as Baudelaire would have done on similar occasions—on a scrap of Parisian note-paper :

Moulin-Rouge, May 22, 1892. She danced before the mirror ; the orange rosy lamps. The tall slim girl ; the vague distinction of her grace ; her candid blue eyes ; her straight profile. She wore a tufted straw bonnet, a black jacket and dark blue serge skirt—white bodice opening far down a boyish bosom. Always arm in arm with another jolly girl, who also seized my arm—for the invariable reason of giving them drinks. The reflections—herself with her unconscious air, as if no one were looking—studying herself before the mirrors. The horrible little creature with black hair turning all by herself in the middle.

Only La Mélinite—her actual name was Jane Avril —had a perverse genius ; besides which she was altogether adorable and excitable, morbid and sombre, biting and stinging; a creature of cruel moods, of cruel passions; she had the reputation of being a Lesbian; and, apart from this and from her fascination, never in my experience of such women have I known anyone who had such an absolute passion for her own beauty. She danced before the mirror under the gallery of the orchestra, because she was *folle de son corps*; because she had *une folie dans l'âme*. She was so incredibly thin and supple in body that she could turn over backward—as Salome when she danced before Herod and Herodias—until she brushed the floor with her shoulders.

One reason why Lautrec painted so many portraits of her was because she remained *une grande amoureuse des ateliers*, and another because she obeyed all the painters' caprices, and another because she was all fine nerves, and as passionate as abnormal. Did she appreciate Lautrec's genius? I imagine that she did, because she loved the odour of painting.

Lautrec's coloured poster of *Jane Avril* (1899) that hangs on one of the walls of the study in which I write, is simply magnificent. She is painted with his feverish colours; she stands sideways; an immense hat flaps red wings of wild birds striped with black, vanishing into space, over her bright yellow hair; her red mouth, fine nose and perverse eyes glitter before me; her hands are extended on either side with two sweeping gestures; and—so like the depravity of Lautrec—a living cobra writhes around her body. His evil mouth whose tongue hisses is painted in yellow and red and thin black colours; it seems to dart at her chin; and this adorable and fearful monster's body is painted

23

with yellow that verges into pale blue, mixed with a peculiar kind of green ; and, the more he coils around her, the more violent are his colours. And—a certain sign of Lautrec's perversity—he has inserted on the right, near the bottom of the poster, the most inhuman and delicious and exotic and tiniest of snakes who absolutely flies in the air, lifted by a delicate wind.

Certainly, Lautrec realizes his dancers, and realizes them as no one else did before him—leaving aside Degas. They are Lautrec's by right of possession, by right of his malignant and pitiless genius ; he loves them after his own fashion ; they love him after their own fashion : two utterly different kinds of love ; and even the atrocious Goulue was obliged against her will to be aware of this vivid love of his.

VII

THE *chahut* is the successor, one might almost say the renaissance, of the *cancan*. Roughly speaking, the *cancan* died with the Bal Mabille, the *chahut* was born with the Jardin de Paris. The effervescent Bal Bullier of the Quartier Latin, in its change from the Closerie des Lilas, of the days of Murger, may be said to have kept the tradition of the thing, and, with the joyous and dilapidated Moulin de la Galette of the heights of Montmartre, to have led the way in the establishment of the present school of dancing. But it was at the Jardin de Paris, about the year 1884, that the *chahut*, or the *quadrille naturaliste*, made its appearance, and, with La Goulue and Grille-d'Égout, came to stay. The dance is simply a quadrille in delirium—a quadrille in which the steps are punctuated by *le port d'armes*

24

(or high kicks), with *le grand écart* (or " the splits ") for parenthesis. *Le port d'armes* is done by standing on one foot and holding the other upright in the air ; *le grand écart* by sitting on the floor with the legs absolutely horizontal. Beyond these two fundamental rules of the game, everything almost is left to the fantasy of the performer, and the fantasy of the whirling people of the Moulin-Rouge, the Casino, the Jardin de Paris, the Elysée-Montmartre, is free, fertile, and peculiar. Even in Paris you must be somewhat ultramodern to appreciate it, and to join, night after night, those avid circles which form so rapidly here and there on the ball-room floor, as a waltz-rhythm ends, and a placard bearing the word " Quadrille " is hung out from the musicians' gallery.

Of all the stars of the *chahut*, the most charming, the most pleasing, was La Goulue. Still young, though she has been a choreographic celebrity for seven or eight years ; still fresh, a veritable " queen of curds and cream " among the too white and the too red women of the Moulin-Rouge ; she has that simple, ingenuous air which is, perhaps, the last refinement, to the perverse, of perversity. To dance the *chahut*, to dance it with infinite excitement, and to look like a milkmaid : that, surely, is a triumph of natural genius ! Grille-d'Égout, La Goulue's companion and rival, was not so interesting. She was dark, serious, correct, perfectly accomplished in her art, and a professor of it, but she has not the high spirits, the *entrain*, the attractiveness, of La Goulue. In Nini-Patte-en-l'Air, a later, though an older, leader of the *quadrille naturaliste*, and, like Grille-d'Égout, a teacher of eccentric dancing, we find, perhaps, the most typical representative of the

25

chahut of to-day. She was not young, she was not pretty, she was thin, short of stature, dark, with heavy eyebrows, coarse, irregular features. Her face was worn and haggard, almost ghastly ; her mouth drawn into an acute, ambiguous, ironical smile ; her roving eyes had a curious, intent glitter. She had none of the *gaminerie* of La Goulue : hers was a severely, self-conscious art, and all her extravagances were perfectly deliberate. But with what mastery were they done, with what tireless agility, what tireless ingenuity in invention ! Always cold, collected, " the Mænad of the Decadence," it was with a sort of " learned fury " that she danced ; and she had a particular trick—the origin of her nickname—a particular quiver of the foot as the leg is held rigid in the air—which was her sign and signature. After these three distinguished people come many. There were La Mélinite, Rayon d'Or, La Sauterelle, Etoile Filante, and many another ; of whom La Mélinite was certainly the most interesting. And then there was La Macarona of the Elysée-Montmartre, whose sole title to distinction existed in the extraordinary effrontery of her costume.

VIII

ON my way to Nini-Patte-en-l'Air's I stopped at a second-hand bookstall, where I purchased a particular edition which I had long been seeking, of a certain edifying work of great repute. Opening the book at random, I found myself at Chapter XX, *De Amore Solitudinis et Silenti*. " Relinque curiosa," I read. Then I put the book in my pocket and went on to Nini-Patte-en-l'Air's.

TOULOUSE-LAUTREC
La Goulue

Of course, I had been at the Trafalgar Square Theatre—two Saturdays ago, was it not?—when the unaccountable British public had applauded so frankly and so vigorously its first glimpse of a *quadrille naturaliste* in England. But now I was going, in response to a special invitation from Madame Nini, to see what I fancied would interest me far more, a private lesson in the art of the *chahut*. I found the hotel, but not, at first, the front door. In the bar no one knew of a front door, but I might go upstairs, they said, if I liked : that way, through the door on the right. I went upstairs, found a waiter, and presently Nini-Patte-en-l'Air bustled into the room, and told me to make myself quite at home. Nini is charming, with her intense nervous vivacity, her quaint seriousness, her little professional airs ; befitting the directress of the sole *école du chahut* at present existing in the world. We have all seen her on the stage, and the little, plain, thickset woman with the vivid eyes and the enigmatic mouth, is just the same on the stage and off. She is the same because she has an individuality of her own, which gives her, in her own kind of dancing, a place apart—an individuality which is reinforced by a degree of accomplishment to which neither La Goulue nor Grille-d'Égout, neither La Sauterelle nor Rayon-d'Or, can for a moment pretend. And I found that she takes herself very seriously ; that she is justly proud of being the only *chahut* dancer who has made an art out of a caprice, as well as the only one who has conquered all the difficulties of her own making, the only executant at once faultless and brilliant. We talked of many things, I of Paris and she of London, for which she professes an immense enthusiasm ; then she told me of her triumphant tour in America, and how she conquered America by the subtle discretion of her *dessous*, which were black. Blue, pink, yellow, white, she experimented with all colours ; but the American standpoint was only precisely found and flattered by the factitious reserve of black. Then, as she explained to me all the technique of her art, she would jump up from the armchair in which she was sitting, shoot a sudden leg, surprisingly, into the air, and do the *grand écart* on the hearthrug. But the pupils ? Oh, the pupils were coming ; and Madame and I had just finished moving the heavy oak table into a corner, when the door opened, and they came in.

I was introduced, firstly, to La Ténébreuse, a big woman of long experience, whom I found to be more supple than her figure indicated. Églantine came next, a tall, strong, handsome, dignified-looking girl, with dark eyes and eyebrows ; she is in her second year, and has been with Nini in America. Then came Épi-d'Or, a timid, yet gay, rather English little blonde, who makes her *début* in London. They sat down meekly, like good little schoolgirls, and each came forward as she was called, went through her exercises, and returned to her seat by the door. And those exercises ! It was not a large room, and when a tall girl lay at full length on the floor, and Nini bent over her, seized one of her legs, and worked it about as if it were a piece of india-rubber, the space seemed quite sufficiently occupied. When Églantine took her third step towards me, kicking her hand on the level of her eyes at each step, I tried to push back my chair a little closer to the wall, in case of accidents ; and the big girl, La Ténébreuse, when she did the *calbute*, or somersault, ending with the *grand écart*, or the splits, finished at, almost on, my feet. I saw the preparatory exercises, *le brisement*, or dislocation, and *la série*, or the high-kick, done by two in concert ; and then the different poses of the actual dance itself : *la guitare*, in which the leg is held almost at right angles with the body, the ankle supported by one hand ; *le port d'armes*, in which the leg is held upright, one hand clasping the heel of the boot—a position of great difficulty, on which *le salut militaire* is a slight variation ; *la Jambe derrière la tête*, a position which requires the most elaborate acrobatic training, and which is perhaps as painful to see as it must be to do ; *le croisement*, which ends a figure and is done by two or four dancers, forming a sort of cross-pattern by holding their heels together in the air, on a level with the eyes ; and *le grand écart*, or the splits, which is done either by gliding gradually out (the usual method), or by a sudden jump in which the split is done in the air, and the body falls violently to the ground, like a pair of compasses which have opened out by their own weight. It was all very instructive, very curious, very amusing. " Relinque curiosa," said the book in my pocket. But I was far from being in that monastic mood as I watched these extraordinary contortions, done so blithely, yet so seriously, by Ténébreuse, Églantine, and Épi-d'Or ; Nini-Patte-en-l'Air giving her orders with that professional air now more fixed than ever on her attentive face. It was all so discreet, after a fashion, in its methodical order ; so comically indiscreet, in another sense. I am avid of impressions and sensations ; and here, certainly, was a new sensation, an impression of something not easily to be seen elsewhere. I sat and pondered, my chair pushed close back to the wall, Nini-Patte-en-l'Air by my side, and before me Ténébreuse, Églantine, and Épi-d'Or.

IX

TURN, now, to some of Lautrec's *chahut* dancers, and realize that they were much more real than reality, much more unreal than they actually were ; as abnormal as the Russian dancers.   Only, the Parisian dancers rhythmed the Sexes—abominably and astonishingly and incredibly.   What did the Moulin-Rouge contain ?   The Sexes, and the very heat and the odour of them.   Again, what did these dancing women do ? Almost everything except being perfect in art ; and, for the greater part, it was an unashamed exhibition of their legs, of the naked skin shown above their stockings when they flung their legs at arm's length from their heads, and when they did the *double splits*.

Still, to have seen them dance night after night, and to have cried at them—as I always did in Spain—*La Mélinite ! La Goulue !* these are what one wanted in the response of their malicious eyes and in the perverse malice of their smiles.   And to have seen Lautrec there, as I have said, night after night, watching them, drinking and smoking with them, drawing them : there also, one got what one wanted ; and, often enough, much more than one wanted.

Lautrec's *Les Valseuses* torments my imagination ; for I feel as I always felt in Paris, in these Music-Halls, the exasperation of the Flesh, the suffocating atmosphere. Here, in the Moulin-Rouge, he fixes one's vision on two enigmatical women who dance, slowly, sensually, seductively. Among those who are seated in the low gallery railed off from the floor, one sees La Mélinite, adorable, magically fascinating.

La Goulue au Moulin-Rouge shows one corner of the Music-Hall. Her dress very low at the back, her left hand pressed firmly on her waist, she is arm in arm with Messalina, a monstrous beast, a Vampire, who gloats over her ; the type, certainly of one of the worst forms of degradation, a figure of Incarnate Evil, a Beardsley and a Rops ; tainted with an unspiritual corruption ; a satire on her own sex ; an adder-tongued Agrippina. Lautrec, whose genius has in it Latin roots, exhibits in I know not how many of his magnificent and abnormal paintings a sense of satire as primitive and as elemental as that of Aristophanes and of Rabelais, of Swift and of Juvenal. I am certain that deep down, in perhaps the deepest depths of this extraordinary man, there was that indignation which drives such artists to create—*facit indignatio versum*, as Juvenal said. In his heart-rending mockery, Lautrec —when he most hated himself—created deformed monstrosities ; where, for instance, some abortion of man or monkey is made to read an abominable book : in bestial stupidity—the symbolism of an evil genius.

Départ de Quadrille is magnificent : in this enormous picture he gives a revelation of one particular corner of the Moulin-Rouge almost under the orchestra, where the avid circles formed, as one's excitement increased ; where, in fact I, being tall, could easily look over the heads of the others. Suppose it is Nini-Patte-en-l'Air who stands planted firmly on both legs held wide apart as her wrists press her petticoats against her sides ; planted, like some living tree, she waits, evil-

31

eyed, implacable, for the music to begin. Lautrec
paints the adorable Mélinite, dressed fashionably—
with her curved nose, straight chin, thin red lips,
black eyes—eyes nervous and erotic, perverse and
passionate. She wears her dainty hat with fine
feathers, the white brim shading her forehead and her
thick black hair ; and that elegant robe she is so fond
of, in which he drapes her as if she were his model ;
the right hand just lifts the upper part of her skirt
—to avoid the dust—as any Parisian lady might. But,
for some reason of his, Lautrec places on her left
Félix Finion. " *C'est un cerveau froid*," said Remy
de Gourmont, " *cet homme qui s'est donné l'air d'un
Méphistophélès Americain eut le courage de compromettre
sa vie pour la réalisation des plans qu'il jugeait peut-être
insensés.*"

La Promenade ! How well I remember that Promenade in the Moulin-Rouge ; monstrous, fascinating,
perilous, insidious. Olivier Métra conducts his blar-
ing orchestra to the sound of his dance-music, Le
Mélinite dances with an extravagant ecstasy, twisting
for once her tiny feet *à rebours*—so as to give one the
effect of a modern and no less magical Salome. In her
direction stalk two Jews—with visages devoured by
degradation and debased cruelty. I see stalk in another
direction one of Lautrec's malign women—the women
I always had an intense aversion for. With black hair
under a flapping flat hat, with a man's more than a
woman's long jacket, with a less than womanly trail
of her elongated skirts behind her—she advances,
alone, menacing ; a plague and a pestilence.

In *Femme en Clownesse* Lautrec conceives something abominable, infamous, satirical ; there is in it

much of his contempt, hatred, love, disgust, of this fatal and fascinating abode of Sin. It is one of his obsessions : all this *maquillage* so seductive and so Parisian, this perversity ; an obsession also, of that kind in which one longs to forget oneself—to mix in a moving multitude.

> Is misery most of miseries miserable,
> Or the one flower of ease in bitterest hell ?

Powdered, painted, atrocious and gluttonous, no Messalina but a veritable Clown-woman, a Tribade, she is arrested in her movement ; she turns her body sideways, with her open bodice and naked arms. She has the utter indifference of the animal. By way of contrast, Lautrec introduces, next to her, La Goulue's ugly sister. In another of his pictures he represents a Herod-like Pantomime King, seated on his throne, who holds a sceptre ; beside him, with a sinister face, the Pantomime Queen. Sardonically, Lautrec introduces into his composition a hideous dwarf seated on a stool, dressed in a weird costume—the Personification of Evil.

Fin de Siècle ! An epithet one must always use in regard to Degas, whose genius remains inexplicable ; after him, Lautrec, next in genius ; third, Beardsley, with the fascinating perversity of his limited genius ; fourth, Rops, impure, obsessed by forms of evil, whose Flemish and Hungarian blood infused into him an almost venomous imagination. All these, in different ways and in different senses, visualized the spectacular Vices, and their obscenity ; which was, to Lautrec as to Degas, a clean thing when you touch it with clean hands, a thing elemental ; a thing Rops and Beardsley always deliberately deformed. So, in this dwarf, Lautrec represents one of the leering dwarfs, the "monkeys" by which the mystics symbolized the earthlier vices ; those immense bodies swollen with the lees of pleasure, those cloaked and masked devils shuddering in gardens, and smiling ambiguously at interminable toilets, that are part of a symbolism which loses nothing by lack of emphasis. And so a more profound spiritual corruption, instead of being a more " immoral " thing than the pestiferous humanity that neither begins with Hogarth nor ends with Rowlandson, but which exists between the gutters and the stars, can be, in some senses, moral ; can, even, at times, bring about the triumph of the spirit over the flesh ; evil justifying evil ; that is to say, by the affinity of the stars with the gutters that breed corruption.

X

I met Lautrec, for the first time, in the Moulin-Rouge on a night of June in 1890 : he was seated at the special table that was always reserved for him ; with him was La Mélinite, who had the beauty of a fallen angel ; she was exotic and excitable. No one who was acquainted with Toulouse-Lautrec could ever forget him : nor have I ever seen a man so extraordinary and so sinister as he was. Every night one came on him somewhere in Paris, chiefly in Montmartre, in the streets, in the cafés, in the theatres, in the music-halls, in the circuses. He walked, his huge head lowered, the upper part of his body which was in perfect proportion leaning heavily on his stick ; he stopped—owing to the difficulty he had in walking —stared this way and that way ; his black eyes shone

34

furiously, eyes that amused themselves enormously; he began to speak in his deep biting voice and always in some unimaginable fashion—jests or jokes or bitter sarcasms, or single phrases, in which each word told; simple and brutal, mocking, serious and sardonic.

Son Portrait, par lui-même, seizes one almost literally by the throat; so absolute is this Creator's image of himself; a face malignant and diabolical, sinister and sardonic; with the huge mass of tormented hair that straggles across his high forehead; his tenebrous black eyes; his black moustache; the ironical curve of the lips; the virile nose, strong chin; in a word, the pure aristocrat. Yet, the deeper I gaze into this face that surges out of the void, the more vividly and violently arises the glittering genius of this evil-starred man. So intensely alive is this marvellous image, that lives, breathes, vibrates to every sensation, that has on it all the untamable violence of the animal, the nerves that distort, the cruel craft that connives in all forms of sin and of vice—that, were one's imagination strung to such a point that it might for one instant awaken the dead to life—Henri de Toulouse-Lautrec would be beside me and La Mélinite in the Moulin-Rouge.

Lautrec had a sinister silhouette; and this unbiassed, scornful intellect, which had worn many masks and many disguises, concealed in itself an immense contempt, an inhuman mockery, and an elemental sarcasm. He was consumed by a continual protest, an insatiable thirst, condemned as he was, tortured as he was, to be a man whose genius was prodigious. His passion for life and for at times living in the life of others aided him in his creations. His biting irony,

his diabolical wit, his fierce gestures, his deep-throated
intonations, his furies, his frenzies, caused him to
assume an attitude of defence against certain attacks
which infuriated him.

Lautrec could wrench a grandeur out of crime, and
he could uplift mere crime to the height of Tragedy.
Out of materials no one ever used before him he would
create types of the basest forms of humanity—the most
degraded types of animality, the impression of which is
single, intense and overwhelming. His genius was
splendidly spendthrift. He could construct, from his
vision, characters—real or imaginary—of whom we are
told nothing, of whose thoughts we are unaware; he
would reveal the infinitely subtle mesh of intricate
movement or emotion; he would make manifest, in
their actions and in their faces, their souls, where the
soul's life in reality exists. And that was only one of
his infinite manifestations : it is a spectacle of life we
are beholding : and life in action.

To have seen Lautrec at the *Rat Mort* or at the
Café de la Place Blanche was in itself a revelation.
There he would be hidden always in the crowd, but
very much at his ease—he loved crowds; and there
he would design certain criminal faces and grimaces,
certain dancers of both sexes, ready for the Quadrille
or in the act of dancing; now, as he had a way of
doing, moving along the floor, now seated drinking at
small tables; always with his invariable indications
of the thumb and the pencil, and with his peculiar
retouchings, as he hastened to finish them.

Besides his physical singularity that made him so
conspicuous, there was something bizarre in the way
he wandered; one never knew where he wandered

36

nor where to find him, so immensely changeful he was, and in his curiosity so insatiable, that to him, as to the Spaniards, time meant nothing ; and one never knew if he slept by day or by night. He lived then in la rue Fontaine ; and as night crept over Paris he and the others—one never quite knew who the others were—haunted *Le Clou*, avenue Trudaine, kept by the noisy Sarrazin, where many of Lautrec's drawings were lost.

Certain of Lautrec's pictures must be seen under a double impression, surging from the extreme and dolorous acuteness of his vision and from the singular fashion in which this vision is rendered. This mixture of acidity and of sweetness, of cruelty and of tenderness, gave to his most ardent admirers an actual enchantment. So, in a curiously different fashion, do certain creations of Michelangelo, which excite and surprise us ; and their strangeness must be sweet also —a lovely strangeness. " And to the true admirers of Michelangelo," says Pater, " this is the true type of the Michangelesque sweetness and strength, pleasure with surprise, an energy of conception which seems at every moment about to break through the conditions of lovely form, recovering, touch by touch, a loveliness found usually only in the simplest natural things—*ex forti dulcedo*."

Only, while Lautrec almost always regards the human model, and especially the women, with a kind of sadness at times injurious of which he seems suddenly to repent as he gives to the line he designs a caressing flexibility, which is, as Verlaine might have said or sung, a prayer to be pardoned ; Michelangelo regards the unveiled human form with no passionate adoration, rather, with an intense pity ; as in so many of his *Pietàs*—the pity of the Virgin Mother over the dead body of Christ, the entombment with its cruel hard stones—that is the subject of his predilection. Lautrec knows how to disengage—as by some alchemist's subtle and secret skill as he dives into the uttermost depths of the hell that is man's heart, that is woman's heart—what is desolating and lamentable in the corrupt and tainted graces of hectic women, " sad with the whole of pleasure," which is their fashion of sinning, of repenting, of perfuming with precious oils their despoiled bodies, of becoming, as it were, clairvoyant.

For sheer malice no one excelled Lautrec : it was one part of his sardonic and satirical and ironic genius, that, added to his animality, excited him to certain creations never yet conceived, out of an imagination so extraordinary and so absolutely sure of itself, that no one can dispute the certainty of his execution. His mastery of his material is inflexible ; the accuracy of his drawing, when he is not drawn aside into eccentricities, is undeniable ; the purity of the outlines— the vaguely coloured outlines of the curves of a Circus arena, the superb anatomy of a horse, the astonishing perfection of the drawing of the tall girl who stands at the end of the tight rope, one foot before the other, her hands behind her back holding on to the wooden prop made to support her before she begins to balance herself—is miraculous. And in the green *décor* that evokes the very atmosphere of a haunted hell, where one sees the lighted globes as if they were three gold stars, the figure of the girl stands out—a figure fearless and feminine—in her faultless proportions.

XI

IT has often been asked : What is the origin of the Coloured Poster ? No one knows its origin. Some suppose the germ may be found in a papyrus dated 146 B.C., among the collections of the Louvre, which deals with the escape of two slaves from Alexandria ; another, not so ancient, is an inscription in Greek issued under the reign of Herod the Great, which forbids, under the pain of death, the entrance of strangers into the Temple of Jerusalem. There were the signboards of the Middle Ages, the public criers in Berry in the year 1141 who went about the taverns carrying with them wares they had on sale. The earliest English poster might be that by which Caxton in 1480 summoned the " Pyes of Salisbury " at Westminster. There is a royal proclamation of the famous François Premier in regard to the Paris police, which was *attachées à un tableau, escripter en parchemain et en grosse lettre*, and was certainly an *affiche*.

The modern artistic poster movement began in 1836 with one done by Lalance as an advertisement for *Comment meurent Les Femmes* ; which was followed in 1837 by Célestin Nanteuil, an advertisement for *Robert Macaire*, done before he began his famous illustrations for Balzac and for Gautier. Next comes Gavarni, with his series of *Les Affiches Illustrés* : next comes Manet with his atrocious and almost obscene *affiche* for *Les Chats* of Champfleury—which represent in an Oriental fashion a black and a white cat with lifted tails almost in the act of love-making under the glimpses of a grotesque moon.

The Parisian Poster was literally invented by Jules

39

Chéret ; in Paris he was called *le roi de l'affiche*. He had the instinct of rapid movement, a colourist's temperament, a certainty of design, and with this a subtle sense of women's fascinating poses, and of splashing the hideous and naked walls of Paris with amazing improvisations and with an immense gaiety ; as in his *Entrée des Danseuses* and in his *Cascade de Clowns*—the phrase of Huysmans who had an inordinate admiration for his designs. So had all of us who haunted Paris in those years for his fiery yellows, uncompromising greens, furious reds and leaden blues —riots of colour, bewildering and at times baffling to one's vision ; for his figures seem to rush this way and that way in a kind of dazzling disorder ; he who could symbolize dancing, pantomime, comedy, music ; he who had that peculiarly French characteristic of being *chic*, as in his coloured *affiches* of the Alcazar d'Eté, the Folies-Bergère and the Moulin-Rouge.

Suddenly, with his sinister genius, surges into the midst of these minor stars, Toulouse-Lautrec. In 1892 he sent to the *Salon des Indépendants*, *L'Affiche pour le Moulin-Rouge*. After this he used more violent and more complicated colours, the foundation generally in green on white paper ; the tones blue, yellow, red or black. Among these are *Le Pendu*, *Le Divan Japonais* (75 rue des Martyrs), which shows Jane Avril in profile ; *Aristide Bruant aux Ambassadeurs* ; *Jane Avril au Jardin de Paris* ; *Caudieux*, finally *Babylone d'Allemagne*, equally bizarre and venomous. I have been turning over the pages of *L'Escarmouche*, a satirical journal edited by Ibels and Darien that began in November, 1893, and ended on the first of January, 1894, which contains thirteen fantastic designs of Lautrec. These sentences are worth quoting : *M. de Toulouse-Lautrec, le collaborateur assidu de ' l'Escarmouche,' met la dernière main à une affiche (Colombier) répresentant le chansonnier Bruant, et qui fera sensation. Ajoutons que ' le Divan Japonais ' a eu le bon goût de confier l'exécution à M. de Toulouse-Lautrec, qui sut, à son habitude, en faire une merveille.*

Caudieux (1893) has in it all Lautrec's malignity, as he makes this hideous *cabotin* strut across the stage of a music-hall, all animated and animal action, legs and arms that gesticulate ; puffed cheeks and ogling eyes that give him rather an absurd resemblance to Oscar Wilde at his worst. *Au Pied de l'Echafaud* has the monstrosity of the *Mahouin* of Villiers : the condemned criminal, with the visage of an utterly debased brute, with naked throat, thrust forward by the executioner who lays one heavy hand on his left shoulder ; one sees part of the guillotine and that awful hole in the wooden plank through which his head must be inserted ; a ghastly thing ; only Lautrec, with his sense of pity, shows one the priest behind him who carries in his hands an open Latin Bible.

In *Le Rire*, January, 1897, there is a splendidly ironical caricature which is transformed into a Poster by Lautrec of Baron, in *Les Charbonniers*, who seems to be saying : *Monsieur le secrétaire de Monsieur le Commissaire !* Above is printed : *Les journaux annoncent que M. Baron, l'illustre comique, quitte prochainement le théâtre des Variétés, où il a remporté de si retentissants succès.* With a lawyer's cap on his head, with heavy eyelids and sombre eyes, with an ugly nose, a long mouth covered by a black moustache, with an upright collar that touches his upper lip, he looks at one sideways, with a most comical gravity. He sits there alive as life, drawn with amazingly pure dashes of the thick pencil. Lautrec's abrupt vision seizes this Cabotin and seems to fling him at you—with hatred and with a secret malice. Just then Lautrec was one of the many Parisian celebrities who were on the jury of *Notre Concours de Masques au Bal de l'Opéra*, which took place on the thirteenth of February. Among the others are Willy, Willette, Jules Renard, Arsène Alexandre, Tristan Bernard, Georges Courteline—who happened to be alive. The *Gil Blas Illustré*, a risky and frisky journal, gave many of Steinlein's pitiless and relentless coloured illustrations, whose *métier* is to add his ironic cruelty to all of his designs in which vice and squalor are shown—as he shows them in his Posters—in their tragic comedy. I prefer far and away to these some splendid posters of Anquetin, a friend of Conder's and of mine, who has a prodigious talent ; as in the design on the cover of the first number of *Le Rire,* in which he represents a figure of a man in a mediaeval costume—with the grotesque and laughing face of Cyrano de Bergerac—who points with his nervous hands to the grimacing pygmies who form a crowd in some square in Paris. After Anquetin comes Métivet, whose Poster of Eugenie Buffet, as she stands outside *Les Ambassadeurs,* a menacing and nocturnal and shivering figure, is, in its originality, sombre ; she is even more tragic and depraved, with her passionate and desperate eyes, when she stands outside *La Cigale* (24 Boulevard Rochechouart), defiant and undaunted ; behind her one sees in a vision a glimpse of part of the Windmill of the Moulin-Rouge, or, it might be, of the Moulin de la Galette.

XII

IN June, 1920, I turned over Lautrec's lithographs in
the Bibliothèque Nationale ; there are more than
three hundred of them. The first I came on was :
Exposition du 20 Avril au 3 Mai, 1903, 52 rue Lafitte.
On the cover is a superb naked woman, sensual, sublime in degradation. She stares at one with a gesture
like one of Rodin's women, the woman-animal with
sleepy eyes ; and, in her, some of the perversity of
Baudelaire. It is interesting to compare these versions of a subject which so many artists have treated,
always in a spirit of perversity, from Hieronymus
Bosch, with his swooping and crawling abortions, to
Rops, with his woman of enticing flesh spread out
mockingly upon the cross, from which she has cast off
the divine body. In one of these lithographs, a man
with his arms on a table has almost the naked face of
Balzac : it reminded me of a Daumier.

Daumier's genius was immense ; Baudelaire, with
his infallible instinct, attributes to him " the strange
and astonishing qualities of a great genius, sick of
genius." Essentially dramatic, his effect is the angry
assault of the nerves on his matter—in which he is so
curiously like Lautrec—and the tilt of the lance against
the windmill : in a word, a Cervantes who paints.
In both the moralist is always awake ; both are haunted
by the sense of sin, of sin's punishment ; of guilt and
of crime ; both are violent, both satirical. And it is
in Baudelaire's praise of Daumier that I find what
might almost have been written on Lautrec. " Daumier's design is naturally coloured. His woodcuts and
lithographs give one the sensation of colour. His

43

pencil can convey anything it likes to—black over white. He knows how to divine colour like thought, which is the sign of supreme art."

As for *Elles*, they are astounding. Here is a cocotte before a mirror, who is doing up her hair ; a man's top hat lies on a table beside her bed. In another a woman stoops over a bath, she pours in water out of a tin can ; the effect, in these pale colours and in the body's outlines, is amazing. A gorgeous half-naked girl shows one breast as she bathes her back ; she reminds me of a Degas. Next I come on a girl cruelly caricatured, huddled against her bed, half out of it ; she has sullen sly eyes. This, apart from the caricature, reminds me of a pencil drawing of Blake I have before me ; where Blake himself seems to be lying in bed, one arm and hand laid on the bedclothes, as she, lovely and slender, with her hair down her back, her chemise rolled round her waist, sits on the edge of the bed, the right leg curved over the other that she holds in her left hand, the foot just touching the knee of the other leg, with a wonderful stooping gesture.

Superb and unsurpassable is Lautrec's design of a dainty girl in bed, lazy and luxurious, full of sleep, sombre and sensual. *Étude de Femme* is exquisite and cruel : this purely outlined impure girl, thin, irritating, in the act of slipping off her chemise, with a kind of daintiness, before she gets into bed. *Le Sommeil* is superb ; it shows a half-naked woman in a state of stupor. She might, for all I know, dream of this sentence of Baudelaire : " Quand je dis que je dormeral demain matin, vous devinerez de quel sommeil je veux parler."

Les Folies-Bergère de M. Prudhomme, a thing

Petronius must have seen in Rome, seen and laughed at, using it in one of the lost chapters of his *Satyricon*, after some revel with Nero and Agrippina and Messalina, shows three masked cocottes dressed in shameless costumes, hudded together in a vivid pose (all in black and dead white) who endure their ghastly existence. Behind them a half-veiled naked statue stands in a half-innocent attitude of frightened shame. It is a Molière in masquerade.

Sarah Bernhardt dans Phèdre is terrific—she, a shadow of guilt made mercenary by lust of forbidden love and furious by her anguished sense of unachieved desires. Guitry is one huge black heap, such as one imagines in that oppressive heat when August twilight merges into night ; he is not even the mockery of a malignant shade ; but, as one struck suddenly with an intense horror of her, his blood surges into his cheeks. And she, this perverse Jewess, poses, wide-eyed and wide-mouthed, with her eloquent lips that seem about to utter Racine's frenzied lines.

Au Théâtre Libre : Antoine dans l'Inquiètude is magnificent ; he has a beaked nose and huge wary eyes, his coat up to his shoulders, hand in pocket —intensely living ; an ardently designed woman holds up a lighted lamp not far from his face. The whole thing gives one a sudden shudder, a sense of suspense, at this tragically dramatic moment of the play, when certainly a crime is going to be committed. Here in the narrow room where the very air breathes murder and all hangs on the suspense of the next moment, these two figures surge out of the void : and, as it were, with some far-thoughted reflection of the blindness of Fate, and of Death's ignobility.

Suppose that, like the dramatists, Lautrec is attracted by some particular soul : the problem obsesses him, intrigues him—the more abstruse and entangled the more attractive it is to him ; and he begins to reconstruct, before one's eyes, the whole series of souls—in the Moulin-Rouge, or in the Moulin de la Galette or elsewhere—the whole substance of the soul ; but, as he had a passion for deformation, the soul is, so to speak, turned inside out. I have watched him in his studio when he was working at his mental machinery, which he disclosed before me. As for his secrets of Creation, these lived and died in him.

Terror : that was the effect at which Lautrec often aimed : terror standing out vividly against a background of obscure and more than dreadful mystery. The " root of horror " from which the whole thing grows has been planned, one becomes aware, in Hell : do these supernatural solicitings merely foreshadow, or do they actually instigate, the deeds to which they bear witness ? We see in one of his great pictures the absolute imprint of " the Crowned Emperor of the Nether Clefts of Hell "—Villon's—and she shares no resemblance with the other Hecate but her name, and she is more dreadful because she is very human. He has realized how unapproachable is the darkness out of which we have but just stepped, and the darkness into which we are about to pass. Seen against the last horizon of the world, where God and men act out their brief human tragedy, or as if upon a narrow island in the midst of a great sea, these are indeed fatally aware that a few steps this way, or that way, will plunge them into Night Everlasting : always the intervals absorb them as if it were to be Eternity, and we see

them rejoicing and suffering with an abandonment
to the moment which intensifies the pathos of what we
know is futile. Love was to Wagner (what Love
never was to Lautrec) so ecstatic and so terrible, because
it must compass all its anguish and delight into an
immortal moment. That mysterious intensity of appeal
which we see in the faces of Rossetti's and Lautrec's
latest pictures had something of the same appeal as
the insatiable crying out of a carnal voice, somewhere
in the depths of Wagner's latest music. And the
music given to Kundry in *Parsifal* has human blood
in it.

XIII

No painter before Lautrec ever revealed, with such
consummate genius, with such incomparable mastery
of his materials, with so passionate a pity, with so little
reverence for the flesh taken simply as flesh, with so
desperate a sense of the tortures these creatures are
fated to endure, with so pitiless a sense of what one
has *à tuer dans la vie*, and with such poisonous colours
—violent greens and reds and oranges—and yet with
so strange a sense of what can be literally pure in
impurity, those women who meant so much to him.
And he has sealed upon them the sign of their eternity.
These bear upon them the stigmata of their sins.

No poet since Villon has ever spoken for the body
with more simplicity or with a more penetrating
humanity than Verlaine in this great sonnet:

The body's sadness and the languor thereof
Melt and bow me with pity till I could weep,
Ah! when the dark hours break it down in sleep
And the bedclothes score the skin and the hot hands move;

Alert for a little with the fever of day
Damp still with the heavy sweat of the night that thinned,
Like a bird that trembles on a roof in the wind :
And the feet that are sorrowful because of the way.

And the breast that a hand has scarred with a double blow,
And the mouth that as an open wound is red,
And the flesh that shivers and is a painted show,
And the eyes, poor eyes so lovely with tears unshed,
For the sorrow of seeing this also over and done :
Sad body, how weak and how punished under the sun !

In other of his poems it is the voice of the flesh, praying such mad and useless prayers to be delivered, repressed but crying against the spirit, a voice of bewildering temptations, whose deadly savour of delight could but come out of a consciousness of how delightful that sin was of which he had repented. And, just as now and again, some picture of Lautrec actually attains touches of sublimity, so, just as in his supreme sonnets, Verlaine also attains sublimity, we have in these absolute passion, the soul of one who, as Blake said of Santa Teresa, " guides the winepress of love," crying upon God the Trinity with a wild cry : " *Êtes vous fous?* " And as Lautrec can produce beauty out of bestiality, and with pure perfection of Art, so I need only quote Verlaine's famous phrase : *J'ai la fureur d'aimer*, for proof that there is no part of his work which is not the expression of some form of love, human or divine, grotesque or heroic, but always insatiable. " Cependant, la Femme, Lautrec l'ai aimée, adorée, comprise, mieux que personne."

It was said of Lautrec : " Il aurait pu outrer sa nature déjà outracière." Ardent, indefatigable, he divided his life into two parts : one for pleasure and one for work. Virile and voluptuous, his senses were furious and his passions insatiable. He said to me once a phrase I have never forgotten: " Ma Vie, c'est une chose effrénée." And there were times when he abandoned himself to an absolute oblivion of the senses. In him, one saw always the man and the artist. His sense of beauty was extraordinary. And yet how often does one not find in his work this sense of what is infinite in beauty allied with a form of ugliness, which is pardonable because it literally existed in the greater part of his models. And it was with a loving frenzy that he adored the image he made for himself of Supreme Beauty. When he painted he was curiously indifferent to what was beautiful and to what was ugly. He always painted what he saw with his ferocious eyes and his intense vision, " où, plus exactement, tels qu'il les dégagait des apparances, dans la seule verité d'une impression aiguë." No modern Painter, with the exception of Augustus John, left so powerful an impression of his personality. Nor is it to be wondered at that Lautrec's life should be revealed (as far as such lives can be revealed) in his pictures and lithographs, and designs and posters ; and, according to my own impression, what he revealed was as profoundly and passionately the revelation of his stormy existence as when a Poet reveals his intimate life in his poems. And it has been said : " Ce sont de veritables Mémoires sur lui-même que ces tableaux. Il y apparaît tout entier, dans toute sa misère, dans tout son orgueil, presque dans le détail de son existence quotidienne." Think for a moment of Paul Verlaine and of Lautrec. With all the pains, misfortunes and the calamities which followed them step by step in life, I think few men ever got so much out of their lives or lived so fully, so intensely, so passionately, with such a genius for living. That is indeed why Verlaine was a great Poet and why Lautrec was a great Painter. Both were men who gave its full value to every moment, who had out of that moment all that moment had to give them. It was energy, vital and virile energy, the violent force of natures which were always receiving and giving out, never at rest, never passive, or indifferent or hesitating. And there was something curiously alike in their faces : both faces devoured by visions, feverish and somnolent, both intellectually proud, both spiritually defiant : the air of one who remembers, not without an effort, who is listening, half distractedly to something which other people do not hear : coming back so suddenly and from so far, with the relief of one who steps out of that obscure shadow into the noisier forgetfulness of life. And, just as I have seen in Paris, in some café, a profound slumber in the face of Verlaine, with its startling awakenings : so I have seen in Lautrec's studio and in the Moulin-Rouge a more than startling awakening out of the somnambulist's slumber on the face of Lautrec. And there are few poems of Verlaine in which the Soul or the Flesh of the Poet does not seem to speak, and, as he speaks, to sing. Social rules are made by normal people for normal people, and the man of genius (there are limitations of course when one refers to men of genius) is fundamentally abnormal. Lautrec, like the majority of his pictures, was almost entirely abnormal, much more so than Verlaine. Vladimir de Pachman—who has in him Russian and Turkish and French blood—is absolutely abnormal and inhuman, and so he evokes, with this ghostly magic of his, the innermost life of music. He has the head of a monk who has had commerce with the Devil, and it is whispered that he has sold his soul to the diabolical instrument which, since buying it, can speak in a human voice. The playing of Pachman has in it something fantastically inhuman, like fiery ice, and it is for this reason that it remains a thing uncapturable, a thing whose secret he himself could never reveal. It is like the secret of the rhythms of Lautrec's pictures, it is like the secret of the rhythm of Verlaine, and no prosodist will ever tell us why a line like

> Dans un palais, soie et rose, dans Ecbatane,

can communicate a shiver to the most experienced nerves.

Like Guys before him, but with an infinitely greater mastery of his material and a more overwhelming genius, Lautrec painted not only the Vice of Montmartre, but that Vice which is eternal, which has always existed and which is almost invariably seen under the same terms. And, in regard to this modern French equivalent of the Spanish Goya, it only remains for me to add that he is, almost literally, almost inexplicably, as a Painter, the modern equivalent of the Poet Charles Baudelaire. When I reminded Rodin of Baudelaire's profound saying (which applies to all the arts), " L'énergie, c'est la grâce suprême," he accepted the words as the best definition of his own meaning. His *Gates of Hell* are a headlong flight and falling, in which the agonies of a place of torment, which is Baudelaire's rather than Dante's, swarm in actual movement.

Lautrec, who was not much of a reader, told me of his passionate and intense admiration for *Les Fleurs du Mal* and that the origin of many of his most perverse and imaginary bestial pictures were *Les Femmes Damnées*. And what I have written on Rodin's creations might be applied, almost word for word, to those pictures of Lautrec I have referred to. " And all this sorrowful flesh is consumed with desire, with the hurrying fever of those who have only a short time in which to enjoy the fruits of desire. Their mouths open towards one another in an endless longing, all their muscles strain violently towards the embrace. They live only with a life of desire, and that obsession has carried them beyond the wholesome bounds of nature, into the violence of a perversity which is at times almost insane." And just as Rodin's work is founded on a conception of force (the force of the earth, then the two conflicting forces, Man and Woman, with always, behind and beyond, the secret, unseizable, inexplicable force of that mystery which surrounds the vital energy of the earth itself), so is Lautrec's : and out of these conflicting forces they chose, for the most part, the universal, vivifying force of Sex. And the Woman softly, overcomes, to her own Perdition.

In the poetry of Baudelaire, with which the poetry of Verlaine is so often compared (it might as I have said be preferably compared with the paintings of Lautrec), there is a deliberate science of sexual perversity which has something abnormal in its accentuation of vice with horror, in its passionate devotion to passions. Baudelaire, like Lautrec, brings every complication of taste, the exasperation of perfumes, the irritant of cruelty, the very odours and colours of corruption, to the creation and adornment of a sort of religion, in which an eternal Mass is served as if before

a veiled Altar.   And there is no Confession, there is no
Absolution.

XIV

To the great artist life is indeed a comedy, but it is a
comedy in which his own part is to stand silently in
the wings, occasionally ringing down the curtain.
Every joy and sorrow which he gives to his characters
he has himself felt ; but, his characters once in motion,
he surveys them with the controlling indifference of
Fate.   Lautrec, with, in his regard, a haughty insolence, is too absolutely Parisian to be indifferent to
anything ; for he shows us, for the most part, in his
paintings, exceptionable people, grimacing with the
exterior violence of life with which he has animated
them, seeming to be wonderfully close to us, but at
the best as close to us as the people we pass in the
street, not as the friend whose soul is in our hands.
It might almost be said that this human curiosity was
as great as Balzac's ; but with what a different kind of
curiosity !   Baudelaire dismisses Ingres with this scornful phrase : *Ingres est dénué de ce tempérament éner-
gique qui fait le fatalité de génie.*
Lautrec might have found in this sentence something ominous, something foreshadowing, without
perhaps his actual knowledge of it, what can be suicidal
in such men of genius ; the inability to escape from
the soilures of gross contact ; to escape from one at
least unwearying torture—not the eternal torment of
the damned—but of being unable to overleap the
barrier which shuts one in upon oneself—one's
abominable, animal, adorable and despicable self,
which, even in the fervour of our blood, asserts itself ;

asserts itself to the point of setting before us, literally before us, that abyss which separates " the expense of spirit " from the " waste of shame." Baudelaire, writing on Poe, said :

" Il y a, dans l'histoire littéraire, des destinés analogues, de vrais damnations—des hommes qui portent le mot guignon écrit en caractères mysterieux dans les plis sinueux de leur front. L'Ange aveugle de l'éxpiation s'est emparé d'eux et les fouette à tour de bras pour l'édification des autres. Le Diable entrera par une serrure ; une perfection sera le défaut de leur cuirasse, et une qualité superlative le germe de leur damnation."

This was as certainly the case of Poe as certainly it was not the case of Lautrec. Only, in men of such sinister genius, both fated to expire tragically young, there must be, I imagine, the seed of their damnation. Yet, what certainly applies in an equal measure to the Poet and the Painter, is Baudelaire's definition of the evil power we have within us : " Cette force, primitive, irrésistible, est la Perversité naturelle, qui fait que l'homme est sans cesse et à la fois homicide et suicide, bourreau et assassin." *La perversité primordiale de l'homme !* There, with all the craft of the first created Serpent, speaks the perfidious Tormentor, the pernicious Tempter of our souls and of our bodies : the Devil.

Swinburne said wittily and maliciously : " Heine, the snake of the Hebrew Paradise,"—a " smooth-lipped serpent, surely high inspired,"—was never more inspired by the serpent's genius of virulent wisdom than when he uttered, in a most characteristic hiss of sarcasm, a sentence as conclusive in its judgment as venomous in its malignity, describing Musset before he had reached middle age as " a young man with a very fine career—behind him," *un jeune homme d'un bien beau passé.* So might have hissed, with no less venomous tongue, the slimy snakes personified in the detractors of Lautrec's genius ; for, as one is aware, always some venom is secreted somewhere under the snake's tongue.

Certainly the most magnificent, the most evil, the most perverse, the most passionately created of Lautrec's paintings are to be found in his series of *Les Maisons Closes.* Here his peculiar genius discovered itself ; not even Constantin Guys, who preceded him, had the vision of Lautrec ; whose vision is certainly depraved, but with an astounding purity in its impurity. These paintings were made the subject of reproach to Lautrec who never took the trouble to defend himself against these dishonourable critics, the so-called judges of pictures, whose advice is as useless to men of genius as it is unnecessary. And one supposes these severe judges, who had never enough curses in their mouths for Lautrec, might have deserved such counter accusations as these :

> Grim curses out of Peter and of Paul ;
> Judging of strange sins in Leviticus ;
> Another sort of writing on the wall
> Scored deep across the painted heads of us.

That Lautrec ran great risks in so publicly setting himself to attack those houses that he certainly loved too much, and had reasons enough for hating, is evident enough. Yet—to strain the comparison into a paradox—the same was said against Blake, but Blake defended himself with righteous rage. To take an

instance of this, Robert Hunt wrote in *The Examiner*
of 1808 two columns of mere drivel and more raving,
against " Blake's Edition of Blair's *Grave*." The
notice, is rendered specially grotesque by its serious
air of arguing with what it takes to be absurdity
coupled with " an appearance of libidinousness " (note
this also in regard to Lautrec) which " intrudes itself
upon the holiness of our thoughts and counteracts
their impressions." Here is another specimen : " But
a more serious censure attaches to two of these most
heterogeneous and serio-fantastic designs. At the
awful Day of Judgment, before the throne of God
himself, a male and female figure are described in
most indecent attitudes. It is the same with the
salutation of a man and his wife meeting in the pure
mansions of Heaven." Thus sanctified a voice was
it that first croaked at Blake out of " the nest of vil-
lains " which he imagined he was afterward to " root
out " of *The Examiner*.

The same reviewer says of Flaxman's *Satan Overcome by St. Michael* : " We deferentially suggest to
our gifted Sculptor, whether the calf of the advanced
leg ought not to be more swelled." Observe the
total lack of spelling and the vulgarity of the sentence.
David the French painter he rebukes for not painting
Napoleon taller than he was ; he " ought to have
availed himself of the license of art, to deviate from
visible exactness to Nature."

In Hunt's second attack on Blake he becomes
scurrilous. Blake here figures as " an unfortunate
lunatic, whose personal inoffensiveness secures him
from confinement, and consequently of whom no
public notice would have been taken, if he was not "

(the man's grammar, comments Swinburne, here goes mad on its own account, but what then ?) " forced on the notice and animadversion of *The Examiner* in having been held up " (the case by this time is fairly desperate) " to public admiration " ; such is the eccentricity of human error. After such palpable specimens of the critic's futurity, those against Lautrec must be equally dismissed, into the same dust-bin.

Lautrec's self-indulgence of the spirit and the flesh was notorious ; but never in the whole course of his brief and tragic existence did he lower himself in his own esteem ; never did he abdicate that supreme command of his material in which he proved himself consummate. He had the vices of his generation ; let that pass. That he possessed a certain amount of hidden-away virtue under his vices, is to me incontestable. He had an equal passion as a man and as a creator. Passion let run to seed ; that must have occurred in some of his most morbid years. It is certain that he was subject, as Coleridge was, to certain literal spells, not acting along any logical lines, not attacking the nerves, not intoxicating, but like a slow, enveloping mist, which blots out the real world, and leaves us unchilled by any " air from heaven or blasts from hell," but in the native air of some middle region. I have referred to the Serpent ; perhaps Lautrec went on creating just as a serpent moves, which makes a fulcrum of its own body and seems for ever twisting and untwisting its own strength.

There must always be cruelty in men whose genius is united with various elements. There is more cruelty in the Spanish and Russian nations, together with what is Latin in the Italians, than in other races. The

Italians have no reticence in speaking of what they
feel, and that is one of the things which people mean
when they say that d'Annunzio's writing is immoral.
Well, nature is immoral. Take one of his characters ;
you will not know him if you come on him in the
street ; but his jealousy, or his corrupt love of art, or
his self-pity, will seem to be part of ourselves, seen
in a sinister mirror, if we have ever been sincere enough
with ourselves to recognize an abscure likeness when
we see it.

What is cruel in Lautrec is what is literally Latin
in his race. He desires beauty with the rage of a
lover, he desires ugliness with the hatred of a lover ;
and, to him, Sex is the supreme beauty. The visible
world does not always " exist " for him as an entirely
satisfying thing ; he is easily discontented ; and,
studious of the origin of emotions, he finds them
wholly in the physical action of the senses. Lautrec
might have said with d'Annunzio, " I would that I
could live the whole of life, and not be only a brain."
So the Italian confesses, in his desire to fuse life,
sensual life, and art, the art of the senses.

In regard to this question I give this paragraph that
I wrote in Seville :

" I have always held that cruelty has a deep root
in human nature, and is not that exceptional thing
which, for the most part, we are pleased to suppose
it. I believe it has an unadmitted, abominable attraction for almost every one ; for many of us, under
scrupulous disguises ; more simply for others, and
especially for people of other races ; but the same
principle is there, under whatever manifestations, and,
if one takes one's stand on nature, claiming that what-

ever is deeply rooted there has its right to exist, what of the natural rights of cruelty ? The problem is troubling me at the moment, for I was at a Spanish bull-fight yesterday, and I saw there many things of a nature to make one reflect a little on first principles."

The cruelty of the nerves, the exasperation of the nerves : these are the two primitive qualities that tear at us on both sides ; as much in their reaction as in their recoil. For some of us imagination takes the place of virtue, and vice takes the place of imagination. To be " magnificent in sin " : that it is to return to the poisonous age of the Renaissance ; the age of Cesare Borgia, of the Medicis, of Vittoria Accorambona, of the implacable Princes and the unscrupulous hired assassins. To them no degradation was possible ; guilt changes them but never degrades them : one's sin must be deliberate ; one must march straight to one's end ; and the means must be mortal.

X V

In November, 1892, when I was in Paris I saw in an Exhibition certain pictures of Lautrec, filled with his violent genius of paint, his ardours of the flesh ; a man whose genius has been aptly defined by Gustave Geoffroy as " un observateur très doué et très violent de la basse humanité, tel que M. de Toulouse-Lautrec." Among those was *Celle que se peigne*, incisively designed by Lautrec. She sits, combing her hair, before her mirror ; a woman of ripe, rich, angry beauty, who draws one warm long lock of curling golden hair through her full and sensual lips, biting it with her teeth, which adds some of a tigress's charm to the

sleepy and couching passion of her fair face. She is
no Lady Lilith, such as Rossetti was fain to paint; but
one of her lesser sisters in sin ; whose sleepy splendour,
warm with her wild blood, as her head leans back,
satiate with its own beauty, the eyes with in them
neither hate nor love, but languid with unassuaged
desires, reminds me of these lines :

> She excels
> All women in the magic of her locks ;
> And when she winds them round a young man's neck
> She will not ever set him free again.

Were it worth her while to divide those terrible lips
she might murmur these words in *Mademoiselle de
Maupin*, a book Lautrec certainly adored, for it is the
most exquisite and perfect book of modern times, for
no other modern writer ever described nakedness with
so abstract a heat of rapture as Gautier, only, as to
d'Albert, so to Lautrec, he is the artist before he is the
lover, and he is the lover while he is the artist—" Je
trouve la terre ainsi belle que le ciel, et je pense que
la correction de la forme est la vertu."

La femme assise sur son lit has an intense purity of
design, perfect in composition, full of strange beauty.
One sees this nude in a room in an Evil House, half
naked on her bed, seated sideways in an exquisite
position, one naked leg crossed by another on which
there is a black stocking—one sees the high-heeled
shoe on the floor ; and, cunningly, she holds the other
stocking that covers part of her naked leg in a most
deceptive fashion. This, with her pose, her poise, the
chemise that drapes the upper part of her shoulder,
and, with what is astonishing, the effect of her tangled
black hair—which prevents us from seeing her face—

stark against a pale coloured wall, gives one a sense of absolute satisfaction. It is full of luxury and of an animal repose.

In *La Mie*, Lautrec, in a sense, arrives at the last stair of the spiral staircase by which one descends to Hell. The whole thing is so abominable, so absolute in conception, that this vile man and this vile woman are as it were eternal or infernal types of the Passion Vices; and, in their utter abjectness, their rapacious greed, their surfeited faces, their attitudes of hideous aversion, there is the absolute certainty that this red-haired woman with red lips and averted head and that this brute of a man, whose whole visage is one grimace, whose eyes are deadly and poisonous, are damned souls, ripe for hell's fumes.

Now turn to *Les deux amies*. It is quite beautiful, simple and not impure. The two lovely Lesbians, in their chemise and black stockings, lie on a kind of couch, one with her eyes half closed and her naked arm over her forehead under her waving hair reclines against an immense cushion; the other, just as lovely and perverse as the younger one, reclines, one naked elbow on the couch, showing her naked back, gazes tenderly at the other, her hair tressed and a comb in her tresses. They might be two of *Les Amies* of Verlaine :

> Derrière elles, au fond du retrait riche et sombre,
> Emphatique comme un trône de mélodrame
> Et plein d'odeurs, le Lit défait, s'ouvrait dans l'ombre.

" It was needful," I have said of Verlaine, in regard to certain of his disastrous years, " that all this should happen, in order that the spiritual vision should eclipse the material vision ; but it was needful that all this should happen in vain, as far as the conduct of life was concerned." Now, all this was as needful to the depravity of Lautrec as it was to Verlaine's depravity; in both the material and the spiritual vision clashed. And, certainly, there is as much rage and fury and vehemence, in certain verses of Verlaine as in certain of Lautrec's paintings; both—poet and painter—were amorous of women and of colours and of odours and of the flesh and of the soul, amorous of all one lives for and lives by; amorous of ecstasy, amorous of corruption.

La Leçon de Piano of Lautrec is one of the most wonderful of his creations : the sombre room, transformed into blazes of unimaginable colours : and these two old and ugly women whose contrast is at once amusing and monstrous are invented out of Lautrec's sheer contempt for such beings, out of his subtle malice, out of his enormous sense of satire. That they exist there at all, in that peculiar *milieu*—which might, as I am inclined to believe, be a room in an Evil House—is by no means a miracle : it is, in a word, a transmogrification, after the fashion of Rabelais ; with the same undercurrent of cruel humour and biting sarcasm.

The woman who plays the piano is evidently caricatured ; one sees her grimacing profile, the long lean wrinkled fingers covered with rings, the twisted lace at the end of the sleeve ; the cheeks rouged, yellow and green ; the thick pink ear ; the pale grave colours of the neck under the twisted hair—in which purples are mixed with reds and lavenders in a kind of unnatural contortion ; as, in fact, where the bulges of the huge body are shown with immense dexterity.

As for her dress, that is not easy to describe ; there are thick macabre greens in the voluminous folds, dashed in with zigzags of cobalt and purple. Not only is the painter's sinister genius shown in the woman's figure ; but also in the bizarre piano-stool, in which I find a gorgeous series of discords which really harmonize in a marvellous fashion : these violent reds, orange, blue, pale purple, pale green, that clash as they contrast ; below, where the painting suddenly terminates, there is a vision of Satanical colours. Besides, in the whole composition, I find Lautrec's sense of the corruption of flesh ; besides a kind of decomposition of tones and shapes and colours ; almost a disintegration of the flesh.

The other woman who stands—one hears her sing— shows her wide-opened mouth, with red lips that curve upward in wrinkles to one side of her big hooked nose ; her cheeks are inflated, her eyelids heavy ; the rouge is combined with pale yellows and corrupt greens. Her expression is superb and insolent, haughty and horrible. Decadent and degraded ; an expression, a convulsed face, one can never forget : there is in it such an immensity of meaning, of malevolence, of malignity, that she fairly startles one, as a rouged reptile might.

She is swathed in a bizarre dress where purple shades—degrades rather—into paler purple. A lean wrinkled hand with rich rings on one finger hangs nervously, crooked inward ; it touches the other woman's body ; her body touches the other's. She is a monstrous Messalina, with her almost contemptuously confident smile of the animal's confidence in itself, and in the animalism of others. The face

63

comes forward with an eagerness which has become a habit ; life runs strongly beneath those somewhat gross cheeks, on which the rouge sets its disfiguring stains.

XVI

LAUTREC, before and after he visited Spain, admired Velasquez, Goya and El Greco. Naturally, when he was in Spain, that abnormal quality which in him was predominant, leapt like a flash of lightning to *Los Caprichos* of Goya ; then, like the flash of forked lightning, to the paintings of Domenico Theotocopuli, where one sees the lean face, pointed beard, deep fixed eyes, sallow or olive skin, and the look of melancholy pride. And those faces, inconceivably more so than those painted by Lautrec,—in spite of the tormented imaginations both possessed, and in that exaggeration which has overtaken so many of those artists who have cared more for energy than for beauty—are all nerves, distinguished nerves, quieted by an effort, or intensely disquieted.

In Velasquez's paintings which Lautrec saw in the Prado, he would find, in their emotional quality, in the Spaniard's sense of the shadow upon life, the intolerable indifference of nature, of natural fate, weighing upon these unhappy kings and princes whom he has painted, from their solemn childhood to their mature unhappiness. In Zurbaran darkness swallows daylight ; Ribera lacerates the flesh of his martyrs, and tears open their bodies before us, with almost the passion of Goya's cannibal eating a woman. In Goya we see—as Lautrec must have seen—both extremes, the whole gamut from wild gaiety to sombre horror of the Spanish temperament. The world for him is a stage full of puppets, coloured almost more naturally than nature, playing at all the games of humanity with a profound, cruel and fantastic unconsciousness. Velasquez, we say, is life, but life was what every Spanish painter aimed at, and some surprised, again and again, with fine effect. And all the early Spanish painters are always conscious of human emotion expressing itself actively in gesture—Spanish gesture, of course, which is very different from ours.

In *El Sueño de la razon produce Monstruos*, the 43rd of *Los Caprichos* of Goya, I imagine one of his self-portraits ; but a Goya with an invisible face, in a leaden sleep, his head across his hands on a table. There certainly is the actual man, and, near by, a wide-awakened cat, with transparent eyes, keeps him company, and seems to watch over his repose, waiting until he awakens. Above and around the man the air is filled with the silent and velvety flight of the night-birds : eagles, owls, bats, hawks, beat the air with their heavy wings, bringing the obscurity of their plumage into the twilight, adding more light to the light with their eyes that shine like lanterns, touch the sleeper with the fans of vampires. It is a swarm of dreams, the apparition of those strange monsters that inhabit the depths of midnights, who wander in the shadow like the obscure instincts in the deep depths of our souls.

In these abnormal creations of a man whose genius was more abnormal than normal—for, in spite of living to the age of eighty-two, he had a tormented and tortured and inhuman and diabolical imagination, that fed itself on the forbidden fruits gathered in some

Satanical orchard where the Thessalian witches dance naked as they pluck the poisonous weeds under the astral light of an Asian Astarte, who poisons one's imagination and one's body and one's nerves and one's fibres, a pitiless Goddess, a goblin Goddess, who has been seen, invisible except to those who have vision, watching for newly buried corpses, hungry after their blood, avid of their flesh, a Goddess intolerable and unnatural—one sees reflexes of his wandering existence ; as in his intense passion for woman, for things unearthly and yet abominably alive, for monsters whose birth is unknown, who swarm in chaos, who are hateful to God and are hated by Satan ; and who, on starless nights, alone with his distracted self, distressed in spirit, and haunted by evil hallucinations, set himself to create deformations of animality, animality in its basest deformations.

Baudelaire, whose genius was tainted with Satanism, with diabolical insinuations and with instincts that stirred his flesh and that excited his spirit, had a huge admiration for Goya, " whose great merit," said he, " was to create unimaginable monsters. *Ses monstres sont nés Viables, harmoniques* ; no one was more daring than Goya in the sense of the possible absurd—*de l'absurde possible*. All these contortions, these bestial visages, these damnable grimaces are penetrated with humanity." In Goya there is no seizing on his point of junction between the unreal and the real ; so subtle is he, so transcendant, so complex, so perverse, so hideously haunted by forms whose horror surpasses the tortures of nightmares.

Goya, in a sense that neither Hogarth nor Callot had the capacity of doing, created an unholy marriage between the comedy which is fugitive and the comedy that is eternal. As satirical as Miguel de Cervantes, who created an entire world that had never existed before ; of which he jestingly said that his work was " a dry, shrivelled, whimsical offspring, just what might be begotten in a prison," which may or may not be a mere figure of speech. Certainly Cervantes took a peculiar interest in cases of dementia, and his immortal Don Quixote annihilates Space and Time, his equally immortal Sancho Panza has for his direct lineage— the Romantic Knight of Honour had none—Panurge and Falstaff and Homais ; all unsurpassably comic, all unsurpassably self-conceited ; the two first being inimitable liars and the third being inimitable for his tediousness. Cervantes ranks with Shakespeare as a citizen of the world, a man of all countries and times ; only, Cervantes lives by one universal master-piece and, as for those of Shakespeare, one might as well try to number the stars in heaven.

Goya, almost alone among modern artists, has the love of the unseizable—at times of the impossible and of the inconceivable—and an equal love of violent contrasts ; for his nature had in it an immense, an almost turbulent violence, doubled by his incorrigible animality. Swarms after swarms, wind-tossed, tempest-tossed, of Sabbats and witches and naked girls and tortured monks and abominable assassins, pass and return, pass and return again ; and, with them, slain children whose flesh is being cooked over the fire. *Débauches dû rêve !* Only, one never knows where the man begins and the beast ends, so mixed are those two forms of eternal life : so enormous, so monstrous, so immoral, so insanely Spanish, are his

creations. Take, for example, two figures who fly in
the air ; and think if any other painter could have
imbued their faces with such hideousness, in which
all the vices are written—" scored deep across the
painted heads of them "—as it were in the Hell of
Belus, as it were in the Hell of Eblis.

XVII

THERE was something in Lautrec when he was most
exasperated that was singular, angular, vivid, dis-
cordant, and yet exquisitely fascinating. There was
no harmony in his face, but the dwellers under this
strange mask were three, and the problem was how
they contrived their common life. When his speech
loosened, and threw off what had tied down the very
wings of his imagination, that voice rose and soared,
and seemed to me at times like the wild clamours of
some savage eagle, that shouted and knew why it
shouted, high up in the heavens. When he was at his
best he debated with one, with a certain fury and a
certain conviction, as to the existence of the dregs of
the soul, and as to what is the best intoxication for its
petulance and wonder and mockery, and I have heard
him imagine that one, risen from the dead at the Day
of Judgment, might see an arm that reaches out, and
hides the sea and the stars ; or that one might have
been present when Christ, hanging on the Cross,
laments that the bones of his feet are stretched with
extreme pain. I said to him once that in an ancient
Welsh poem there is a fierce, loud complaint, in which
mere physical likeness and the intolerance of age
translate themselves into a limitless hunger, and into

that wisdom which is the sorrowful desire of beauty. And then we spoke of the mediaeval hatred of winter and cold, with a far more unbounded hatred of old age and sickness and the disasters which are not bred in the world, but in a blind part of the Universe itself; older than the world, as old as chaos, out of which the world was made. Transfiguring things fearful and fervent into forms of pure Beauty, worshipping, as he did, Beauty herself with more than a lover's devout adoration, these fervent and fearful things, turning back upon themselves, become luxurious, assumed women's forms in which one saw revealed, bodily and spiritually, the apparent innocence of the flesh (which is rarely if ever innocent) and the ignorance of the spirit (which is rarely if ever ignorant). And, like Rodin, he is possessed with the desire of seizing the unseizable, the inexplicable force of that mystery which surrounds the vital energy of the earth itself—and out of these forces in the eternal battle of sex he also has chosen for the most part the universal vivifying force of sex. And his women, at their worst, live only with the life of their animal desire, and that obsession has carried them beyond the wholesome bounds of Nature, into the violence of a perversity which is at times almost or literally insane.

Just as Lautrec, who knew Edmond de Goncourt, preferred a certain perversity in Nature, to what in Nature is natural, so both painter and novelist admired passionate and sensuous things, partly for their own sake, partly that they had to be complex with all the complexity of a deliberately depraved instinct. In any case Lautrec possessed in the extreme, what I have always possessed, an unholy fascination for forms of evil, of cruelty, of horror ; for abnormalities, for the exaggeration of things to a point in which one's nerves create their own visions. What is in one's blood, remains there always ; and if cruelty is to be found somewhere in one's blood, there it remains always.

Léon Cladel, who had a touch of tenebrous genius, lived, according to his daughter's *Life* of him, rather an exasperated existence : he was too highly-strung, too morbid, too nervous, to be able to resist so many of his exasperations ; he who wrote with unflagging vehemence on peasants and thieves and prostitutes ; whose work is epic, in certain senses, as in the tumult of his coloured and clotted speech, which tortures the French language. Judith Cladel compares him with Rabelais ; the links with Rabelais are " la recherche du terme vivant, se mise en valeur et en saveur, la surabondance des vocables puisés à toutes sources— la condensation de l'action autour de ces quelques motifs éternels de l'épopée : *combat, ripaille, palabre et luxure.*"

Lautrec's immense originality was so much a part of the man himself yet in certain senses so wide apart from him that the man as one knew him and the painter as one admired him, were in a sense *homo duplex.* Women he loved too much (if that were possible in one's Paris !) and for reasons known equally to himself and to them : occult and abstract reasons, in all conscience ; *Les Filles*, in a word, these Lamias and Cleopatras and Messalinas and Lucrezias and Lesbias and Marcellas, who at least ought to be illegitimately descended from Lilith, whose amorous mouths cry and lie and entreat and deny ; who are made to prey on us and for us to prey on ; as God's animals always must. And, it may be justly said that it is those of us who love them most passionately and who are most passionately loved by them in return, are the artists who love women next to their Art ; who, being poets, sing of them ; who, being painters, paint them ; who, being sculptors, mould them in clay and fix their forms in living marble.

It is impossible to give what one calls the spiciest of the anecdotes that went raging over artistic Paris in regard to this singular—this abnormal—product of nature, Lautrec ; for reasons certainly well known to those who loved him, who hated him. Yet in spite of the conflicting legends that disturbed Paris, but which rarely disturbed him—legends that meant no more to him than they did to Villiers de L'Isle Adam —no modern painter was more popular than he was from la Place Clichy to la Place Pigalle. Always, like Villiers, he was looked upon by most people as an amusing kind of madman, a little dangerous, whose ideas, as they floated freely over the café-tables, it was at times highly profitable to steal. Lautrec's life being exasperating to himself, he loved to exasperate the general public. One anecdote can be given, the meaning of which is, perhaps, occult. One day, in the house of a friend, Lautrec wanders about the ante-room, in the act of leaving, as if he were searching for something he fails to find. Anticipating his friend's interrogation, he says to him, softly : " J'avais un petit bâton ! "

Costly objects, this man of nerves simply could not exist without. And, when he wanted to, he would trail some of them from his studio to one of the evil houses he was frequenting ; these houses of iniquity from which he would emerge into some wintry murk of that city of perdition which is Paris, into a world sin-steeped ; out of a world steeped in sin to some houses of perdition.

As for these infamous Houses of Sin, he knew them and loved them, loved them too much, with no lover's love, but with a love of women's flesh ; together with a desire to escape the horrid crew of daily tiresome deeds, and to find himself in heated and perfumed rooms, where the dim alcoves add their esoteric obscurity to the room's mystery, where the winds wafted themselves down the chimney or through a crevice in door or window ; where he designs all the sins on the walls and their names in scarlet letters. And, where the revels go on all night, and those lost creatures that have their souls to save give themselves, not always ignobly. I think some vision rises in those wild and mad and visionary eyes of his, eyes malign and evil, of something far beyond those tempting sins—these sins for which he pays year by year so heavy a price—of some kind of salvation, of some kind of redemption beyond the grave.

And then, as for his less incomprehensible emotions —one wondered at their very existence : they were so disconcerting, so seductive, so much a matter of mixed sensations, of uncontrollable nerves, of impetuosity of a startling spontaneity : of, at times—to use an extraordinary image—when Lautrec talked, the grip he had on us was as if the body of Rabelais had taken possession of the body of Baudelaire.

XVIII

IT is in regard to Lautrec, whose passions were, I imagine, as uncontrollable as they were varied, that I give these sentences of Swinburne on Beaumont and Fletcher's comedy, *The Captain*:

" The monstrous and abnormal criminality of the almost incredible heroine, Lelia, is more like the impudent fancy of a naughty boy than the corrupt imagination of a depraved man. And the first scene of cajoling in which the woman's magnificent art of passionate hypocrisy is brought to bear upon a half-conscious and half-reluctant victim, is finer than anything I know of the kind in prose or poetry before the advent of Balzac's almighty and ever-living Valerie. Madame Marneffe is as matchless as Madame de Merteuil : but the patrician or the plebeian she-devil of immortal fiction might have given a smile of sympathy if not a hand of sisterhood to the hardly less terrible harlot of an English poet's invention."

" Un grand génie est, dit-on, une espèce de monstrosité. S'il reste grand génie dans sa vie privée, ce n'est plus un homme." This fascinating paradox was written by Baudelaire. Always accused of the immorality of his pictures, Lautrec never troubled himself to answer his critics ; Balzac did, triumphantly, time after time, against those who accused his *Comédie Humaine* of being immoral.

" Facts gathered together and painted as they are, with passion for element," is one of Balzac's definitions of the task he has undertaken. In that phrase I find also a definition of the task Lautrec imposed on himself. There is another phrase to be noted : *La passion est toute l'humanité.* All Balzac is in that phrase.

Balzac—that was his misfortune—consumed his life by burning both ends of it as he burns the ends of the candles he uses as he writes : and by an incessant burning thought about men and women, and a passionate human curiosity for which even his own system has no limits. Lautrec—that was his misfortune—consumed his life by a too burning, a too ardent desire for women, and by an existence so prodigiously self-consuming, that it might be imaged, in Shelley's words, as " the desire of the moth for a star," and by these lines in *Modern Beauty* :

> I am the torch, she saith, and what to me
> If the moth die of me ? I am the flame
> Of Beauty, and I burn that all may see
> Beauty, and I have neither joy nor shame
> But live with that clear life of perfect fire
> Which is to men the death of their desire.

Might not Lautrec have cried, as he heard the pallid hand of death knock on his door :

> Who is there lives for beauty ? Still am I
> The torch, but where's the moth that still dares die ?

Our pleasant sins are the most delightful to recall ; our worst, our deadliest sins, have a distinct taste in them of the Devil that dwells within us. No men of genius I have ever known realized so intensely, so poignantly, and so fearfully, these oscillations—the oscillation of the pendulum over the pit—as Paul Verlaine. For, as Charles Morice wrote :

" Other men ' arrange ' their lives, take sides, follow one direction ; Verlaine hesitates before a choice, which seems to him monstrous, for, with the integral simplicity of irrefutable human truth, he cannot resign himself, however strong may be the doctrine, however enticing may be the passion, to the necessity of sacrificing one to the other, and from the one to the other he oscillates without a minute's repose."

Did Lautrec ever " arrange " his life, take sides ? Never, I imagine ; only with that terrible oscillation that is the penalty such men must endure—not only for the sins they commit, the sins they have committed, the sins they never have committed—but because of the antagonism of spirit and flesh ; and also because life, to certain of the Saints, in so far as it is natural, is evil ; in so far as it is corrected by divine grace, it leaves the human actors in it without merit ; since all virtue is God's, though all vice is man's.

XIX

" CETTE nature ténébreuse, barioléde vifs éclairs : " this phrase of Baudelaire's certainly reveals one of the dominant qualities in Lautrec's genius. Also, in these two sentences : " Les artistes modernes négligent beaucoup trop ces magnifiques allégories du moyen âge, où l'immortel grotesque s'enlaçait en folatrant, comme il fait encore, à l'immortel horrible. Peut-être nos nerfs trop délicates ne peuvent-ils plus supporter un symbole trop clairement redoutable."

Goncourt, in 1890, wrote in his notes in his *Journal* : " Plus j'existe, plus j'acquirs la certitude que les hommes nerveux sont autrement délicats, autrement sensitifs, autrement frisonnants, au contact des choses et des êtres du qualité inferieure, que les femmes qui au fond n'ont que la pose de la délicatesse." To this I add one sentence of Baudelaire : " Les sophistes de l'école négative, qui, à cause de leur incapacité à créer, bafouent la création, en sont maintenant les plus bruyants applaudisseurs."

Just as the uncreative scorn creation, just as the creators scorn the uncreative, so the Sophists, who have declared their doctrines all over the world, have invariably quarrelled over their separate doctrines. With the world of intellectual production, as with that of organic generation, nature makes no sudden starts. *Natura nihil facit per saltum.* That all things fleet away—so said Heraclitus—may startle a particular age by its novelty, but takes possession of it only because all along its root was entangled somewhere among the natural but half-developed instincts of the human mind itself.

" Whether or not the Sophists," wrote Pater," were quite fairly chargeable with that sort of ' inward lie,' just this, at all events, was in the judgment of Plato the essence of sophistic vice. With them art began too precipitately, as mere form without matter ; a thing of disconnected empiric rules, caught from the mere surface of other people's productions, in congruity with a general method which everywhere ruthlessly severed branch and flower from its natural root—art from one's own vivid sensation or belief."

When nothing which happens, happens except under God's direct responsibility, when nothing is said which is not one of your " lines," in the drama which is being played, not so much by as through you, there can be no exteriorities, nothing can be trivial, in a record of life so conceived : so, it seems to me that, in the case of Lautrec as in the case of Saint Augustine, men of intense genius are condemned to endure, from the moment they begin to sin, and to the end of their lives, the burden and the travail thereof.

> O, voice
> Wandering bodiless, between sky and sod,
> Angry and pitiful, a crying uncomforted
> Are you not the crying of the Earth on her outraged bed,
> Against man, who has got her with child, to her father God?

So Lautrec's travail, which was gigantic, soon after that travail had begun its inevitable torture, incited him to enter—as it were, but not for always—on a certain night in June—I forget in what year—one of those " bocards " (brothels) one is so well aware of in Paris ; and, I imagine, as much for the sake of his own sins and of his leman's sins as for his and their particular and sinister and delicate tastes.

> John, Master of the Temple of God,
>   Falling to sin the Unknown Sin,
> What he bought of Emperor Aldobrod,
>   He sold it to Sultan Saladin :
> Till, caught by Pope Clement, a-buzzing there,
>   Hornet-prince of the mad wasps' hive,
> And clipt of his wings in Paris square,
>   They bring him now to be burned alive.
>
> Alack, there be roses and roses, John !
>   Some, honied of taste like your leman's tongue :
> Some, bitter ; for why ? (Roast gaily on !)
>   Their tree took root in devil's dung.

Just as *The Heretic's Tragedy : a Middle-Age Interlude* is of all mediaeval poems perhaps the greatest, as it is certainly the most original, the most astonishing, so Lautrec, thinking likely enough of the Unknown Sin, or of the Corruption of Man's Heart, or of both together, decided once and for all that these Evil

Houses were the Abode of Sin where he chiefly loved
to dwell.

> Who maketh God's menace an idle word ?
> —Saith, it no more means what it proclaims,
> Than a damsel's threat to her wanton bird ?—
> For she too prattles of ugly names.

" Il ne laissera pas de se brûler," writes Arsène
Alexandre, " à le fin, au contact des choses corrosives
qu'il étudie et manipule.   Mais ce qu'il cherche avant
tout, c'est une expression d'art, et des ressources pour
la rendre.   Il cherchera, partout où s'offre à ses yeux,
suivant l'expression des Méphistophèles de Berlioz, la
bestialité dans toute sa candeur, un répertoire de
formes et de mouvements exempt de toute convention."

And, indeed, may it not be asked what is so singular
in all this ?   Simply, an obsession that followed on an
infatuation ; simply that the manner of living Lautrec
so deliberately adopted was bound to ruin—sooner or
later—so enormously gifted an existence.   It is by no
means what one calls the suicide of a man of genius ;
nor could it have been the desire to kill another night
as swiftly as possible.   Nor was he one who was ever
" content to ask unlikely gifts in vain," for he certainly
had all he wanted.   He had an exquisite sensibility,
he vibrated in harmony with every delicate or inde-
licate emotion.

These Profligate Houses !   I use the note of exclam-
ation, not the note of interrogation : one does not
interrogate them ; there is enough in the way of interrogation in their sinister, their at times sordid aspect.
You enter : behind you is Life ; no sooner have you
entered, than before you stands Death.

Certainly these Evil Houses are as inevitable as

Sex ; they are just as immoral as Sex can be at its worst ; they are naturally used for immoral purposes. And, to those who have travelled extensively, with an insatiable curiosity, as I have, there is always a subtle difference to be found in them in every foreign country. There is a subtle difference between those in Paris and in Budapest, in Constantinople and in Seville. These houses, where absolute Immorality exists—for in these morality does not—are, literally, a world within a world —a world that turns on its own axle, as the natural world turns. This world is feared and hated by most women who have the prejudices of their sex. They imagine the men they know to be haunters of harlots ; yet who can object to the *leves amores* of their light-hearted admirers ? They adore scandal, which is to them the breath of their lives. French novels have always the same allurements they used to have : from Balzac to Bourget—from a mountain to a mole-hill— there is choice reading.

As for Lautrec, hurled by disaster after disaster into that tragic and passionate and wonderful, vital and virile life of his, what remains for him except to drink and eat life with the rage of a glutton and with the fearful thirst of a drunkard, then to embrace it, then to violate it ?

After one's passion for women, which is primitive, which is rarely ruinous, comes to certain who are fated to sink under it the base passion for drink. Only late in life did Lautrec drink to excess ; it was in the bars which amused him so much that his greenish eyes would gleam with an ardent covetousness. The more exasperated he became the more he needed these excitements, the more fiercely he imbibed them, his art became more exasperated ; these gave him night-

mares ; and, as Cogniot says : " Curieusement et
frénétiquement, par satisfaction physique et nécessité
intellectuelle, Lautrec lampa toutes les boissons spirit-
ueuses connues." He frequented bars in le rue
d'Amsterdam, des Champs Élysées, l'avenue Mon
Faigne, bar Achille, rue Scribe, or Irish or American
Bar, rue Royale ; these hallucinated him, these sent
the blood to his head. He inhaled the violent perfume
of these haunts, impregnated with alcohol, and with the
odours of the flesh. One bar was situated near the
Folies-Bergère, where between eleven at night and two
o'clock in the morning one saw enter acrobats and
prostitutes, wrestlers such as Raoul, Pons, Laurant,
Vervet. In the bar Achille Lautrec came on jockeys,
escorting their girls who, congested, smoked like chimneys and drank like lamps. After leaving these, or
the music-halls, Lautrec, stupefied, made his way to
the Evil Houses.

X X

ALL Paris that wanted to amuse itself went to the Mirliton to see Aristide Bruant and to hear him recite his
monstrous verses on knaves and thieves and street-
girls ; and, naturally, that kind of excitement fascinated
Lautrec. He came on it suddenly : and, having made
Bruant's acquaintance, made this disorderly tavern one
of his head-quarters.

The verse of Aristide Bruant, written, as it was to
be sung, and before the casual and somewhat disorderly audience of a small *cabaret* near what was once
the Élysée-Montmartre ; written, as it was, mainly
in the slang of the quarter, the uncomely *argot* of those
boulevards extérieurs which are the haunts of all that is

most sordidly depraved in Paris,—this verse is yet, in virtue of its rare qualities of simplicity, sincerity, and poignant directness, verse of really serious, and not inconsiderable, literary merit. Like the powerful designs of Steinlen, which illustrated them, these songs are for the most part ugly enough, they have no charm or surprise of sentiment, they appeal to one by no imported elegances, by none of the conventionalities of pathos or pity. They take the real life of poor and miserable and vicious people, their real sentiments, their typical moments of emotion or experience—as in the very terrible and very blasphemous song of the rain, and the poor soaked vagabond ready to " curse God and die "—and they say straight out, in the fewest words, just what such people would really say, with a wonderful art in the reproduction of the actual vulgar accent. Take, for instance, the thief, shut up *à Mazas,* who writes to his *p'tit' Rose,* asking her to send him *un peu d'oseille* (a little " oof ") :

> Tu dois ben ça à ton p'tit homme
> Qu'a p't'êt' été méchant pour toi,
> Mais qui t'aimait ben, car, en somme,
> Si j'te flaupais, tu sais pourquoi.
> A présent qu'me v'là dans les planques
> Et qu'je n'peux pus t'coller des tas,
> Tu n'te figur's pas c'que tu m'manques,
>   A Mazas.

> Faut que j'te d'mande encor' que qu'chose,
> Ça s'rait qu' t'aill's voir un peu mes vieux.
> Vas-y, dis, j't'en pri', ma p'tit' Rose,
> Malgré qu't'es pas bien avec eux.
> Je n'sais rien de c'qui leur arrive. . . .
> Vrai, c'est pas pour fair' du pallas,
> Mais j'voudrais bien qu'moman m'écrive,
>   A Mazas.

Then there is the decrepit old beggar ; the " lily-livered " creature (*j'ai les foi's blancs*) who laments his useless cowardice in regard to matters of assault and battery, but is candid enough to think that at all events he will come to no violent end himself :

> Ma tête . . . alle aura des ch'veux blancs,

the socialist workman, with his *Faut pus d'tout ça . . . faut pus de rien* ; the street-walker, her lover and her jealousies, the grave-digger, who ends all :

> Comm' des marié's, couverts d'fleurs,
> Tous les matins on m'en apporte,
> Avec leurs parfums, leurs odeurs. . . .
> Moi j'trouv' que ça sent bon, la morte.
>
> J'les prends dans mes bras, à mon tour,
> Et pis j'les berce. . . . Et pis j'les couche,
> En r'inflant la goulé d'amour
> Qui s'éshappe encor' de leur bouche.

You may say that these are not agreeable people to be introduced to, and here is a book, certainly, which it is open to everyone not to read. But such people exist in real life, and they are brought before us here, as they so rarely are in the literature which professes to be realistic, with an absolute realism. Bruant's taste lay in the direction of a somewhat *macabre* humour ; he gave us, by preference, the darker side of these dark and shadowed lines ; but if there was much that he left out of the picture, at all events he introduced nothing into it which was not to be found in the reality which it professed to copy. Compare, for instance, *les gueux* of Bruant with those of Richepin. Bruant was a human document, a bit of crude but exact observation ; Richepin gave us nothing but impossible rhetoric about impossible persons. And who would not give all the pseudo-philosophy, the pretentious and preposterous pessimism of the writer of *Les Blasphèmes* for this little casual, irresponsible moral, the comment on the end of a nameless soldier who had been guillotined for committing a murder :

> S'i's'rait parti pour el 'Tonquin,
> I's's'rait fait crever l'casaquin
>   Comm' Rivière. . . .
> Un jour on aurait p't'êt' gravé,
> Sur un marbre ou sur un pavé,
>   L'nom d'sa mière.

So resigned, in so desperate a resignation under whatever fate may send, are these children of the gutter ; philosophers, in their way, since they can accept fortune or misfortune without surprise, if also without thankfulness. Their resignation, their savageries, brutal affections, drunken gaieties, obscene delights ; all these Bruant has realized and presented in the two volumes of *Dans la Rue*, which sum up, as nothing else in contemporary literature does, the whole life of the streets, where that life is most typical, curious, and interesting, in Paris, along the dreary sweep of the outer boulevards.

It was in April, 1891, that I found myself, for the second time, in Paris, on the way to Spain. The hotel I usually lived in was l'Hôtel Corneille. I went there simply because I loved *la rive gauche* ; and I made the acquaintance of a man of some interest who had long since taken the Odéon, Antoine. He lived in the rue Blanche, and I went there with Mlle Lucie Bournigue Dorny, an actress. There were rumours in the papers that the Théâtre-Libre was dead. Bauer's vindictive article in the *Echo de Paris*, Dorny's conjectures as to whether all were really over, or what was going to happen : should we see Antoine at all ? Our first visit, the empty salle, only the door-keeper there : M. Antoine will be back at six. There were portraits and framed pictures all over the walls, with a few pictures (one by Signac), some medallions of literary men and actors, Catulle Mendès, and others ; some *affiches* of Chéret and Toulouse-Lautrec (Bruant) on the stairs. A small ante-room, the *salle de répétition* inside, with Antoine's little bureau at the side on the way in. We went at two, then to the Salon, and the Taverne Royale, and back at six. Half a dozen actors were there, standing about ; one actress. Before this, we had read the programme of the *tournée*, the list of countries to be visited (nearly all Europe), with certain performances to be given in Paris ; also the list of pieces, written on slips of paper, and pasted on the mirror over the chimney-piece. Presently I was ushered in, and talked with Antoine for a good half-hour. He was ugly, with no good features, no profile, a large nose, a receding chin, bright unflinching eyes, and a mobile, typical actor's face. He impressed me at once : he had enthusiasm and he had judgment ; he was vivid, impressionable, reflective. A thing that struck me was that (though he talked fluently and rapidly and with conviction) he listened attentively to what one said, was anxious to know things about the performance of Ibsen's *Ghosts in Venice*, and other matters about which I talked. He had an intense admiration for Ibsen, and especially for *Ghosts* ; then for Hauptmann. There was a natural pride in what he did, but without illusions ; acknowledging that no impression had been made on the larger public, or other playwrights in general. He had his reasons for giving up the Paris performances for a while. He discovered Ibsen and others, and brought them out ; then came quite a movement among the younger French playwrights, which he encouraged and brought out. That movement had had its course, was at present exhausted. There was the Naturalistic movement, which produced some good plays ; then came the Symbolists, who had not done much for the theatre. Now, he said, he would wait, and see what turns up. And he said all this without the slightest air of discouragement ; with vigour, precision, conviction, talking out of his heart. He discussed general questions as if they were his own, and his own as if they were general questions.

That night I went to Le Mirliton, 84 Boulevard Rochechouart, where Aristide Bruant had a *cabaret*, queer enough then, for outside there was no name, but a vague, suspicious look, and the sound of loud voices. One knocked at the door and it was opened, and the door was shut and bolted behind one. When I got there at ten-thirty, Bruant had not yet come from *Les Ambassadeurs*. It was small, with wooden walls, and a few long plaques in high relief covered one wall, representing wild dancers, a sort of Bacchanalia à la Bullier, with mythological touches. Pictures were all about ; an *affiche* of *Les Ambassadeurs* striking in its sardonic and violent way. Queer things hung from every corner ; and along the ceiling swords, carved images, and other odd ornaments. There was an inner room into which the initiated sometimes retired. On the stroke of eleven Bruant entered, wearing black velvet loose coat and trousers, black top-boots, a red shirt, collar and black scarf. He was clean-shaven, with a powerful face, hair brushed back, fine features, a certain dignity and occasionally a genial smile. He sang his own songs to his own music, in a loud and monotonous voice and without emphasis, always walking to and fro. At times there was a sort of grotesque simplicity in his *macabre* songs, such as *A la Villette, A Biribi, Dans la rue*; songs several of which Yvette Guilbert afterwards sang and transformed into her own exquisite and perverse way of singing, making them her own.

XXI

HERE is Goncourt's impression of the first time he saw Yvette Guilbert, at a dinner given by Jean Lorrain.

" No, she isn't beautiful, a flat face, a nose that has nothing Greek in it, eyes with a wild light in them, eyelids rather Satanical, a heap of reddish hair, low breasts : there's the woman. She has a feverish animation, a vivacity of words vastly amusing. She described the famous lunch Rougon-Maeguat in the Bois de Boulogne, with caricatures of the guests and of the way they jeered at Zola. What is original in her jesting *verve* is that it is modern, it is enamelled with the epithets of symbolical and Decadent Poets, with archaic expressions, old verbs such as ' déambules ' : a potpourri of the Parisianism of the present hour, and of the ancient facetious language of Panurge. When I complimented her on the intelligent manner in which she had said Rollinat's verses, she told me how little success she had, on this very night when she said them, and when some of the audience cried at her during her declamation : *Et la Messe ?* "

This is noted June 28th, 1893. On March 7th, 1895, he notes : " Et la soirée se termine par *La*

Soularde d'Yvette Guilbert, où la diseuse de chan-
sonnettes, se revele comme une grande, une très grande
actrice tragique, vous mettant au cœur une constriction
angoisseuse." After that Goncourt praises Sarah,
" dans sa toilette d'idole, et sa séduction indéfinissable
de magicienne antique."

Yvette is the one woman of genius, of a new startling
kind, among many notable and remarkable persons of
talent. Yvette, within this range that the music-hall
allows her, is a great creative artist ; she creates the
very mood in which one listens to her. You go to any
music-hall feeling in key with the coloured gaiety of the
place, the showy illusions of its lights and dances and
upholstery. Yvette begins to sing, and immediately
the gay world that you see across the smoke of your
cigarette, seems to unmask itself, becomes too suddenly
serious, tragic, a piece of real existence. Her pathos
draws tears, her terror an actual shudder ; when she is
cynical, there is no room in the scheme of things but a
vast irony. When she is most witty and daring, one
seems to breathe the very freedom of Paris. *Les
Ingénues* is a slight study in *Les demoiselles de pensionat*,
or *Les demoiselles à marier*—they were one and the
same ; it is essentially of the genre Yvette Guilbert ; it
is witty, malicious, significant, and rendered with
exquisite skill in the fine shades. But the most remarkable song was Richepin's *La Glu*, one of those
grotesquely tragic songs which are, after all, his finest
successes. Then, indeed, one shuddered, one's very
nerves cried out ; and is not that the aim of the modern
artist in sensations ?

Always Yvette is the same artist ; her art is a very
personal kind of art, but she is a great impersonal

artist, absolutely mistress of herself and of her material. Her voice creates an atmosphere by a single inflexion, her face expresses every mood suggested by her voice. *La Légende de Saint Nicolas* was a quaint, half-childish, and altogether naïve piece, different from anything I have ever heard her sing ; it had some of her pointed simplicity, some of her gravity, some of her mysterious suggestion. " Je suis dans le Bottin," supposed to be said by the man of the world, in *The Directory*, to the man who has not got on in the world (one of Aristide Bruant's monologues), had all the realism of a close character-study, taken directly from life, perfectly imitated, without a touch of exaggeration. *Partie Carée* was very French, very amusing, depending on the naturalness of the rhythm for most of its effect ; it was done with a whimsical chuckling consciousness of its fun and with an admirable gravity. All these were good in different ways, each showed a different facet of her talent, but she was at her best in *Ma Tête*. It is one of those songs of the gutter by which she first made her fame, a song of the gutter in which the gutter remains what it is, and yet becomes beautiful. It goes from the prostitute to the guillotine, and ends with the last convulsive shudder of the head as it falls into the basket. It is a little drama, and every stanza takes one farther along a certain sordid downward way. Every stanza has its own expression, of face and of voice, as the jaunty humour of the beginning fades out of it, and it darkens to the last horror. And it is here, more perhaps than in any of her other songs, that one saw the purity of her art, its fine consuming intensity ; for here was a thing which would be but a masterpiece which she made it, or else gross and vulgar. What she has sung for the most part has been, indeed, " the pity of unpitied human things," as I have elsewhere called it : the pity of vice, of evil, of the misery which men and women make for themselves. Her art, in rendering what is most sordid and most degraded in the world, has always been clean, because compassionate and distinguished, because intellectual. She has made an art of her own which in its own way is a great art. Nothing more deliberate, more finished, more completely achieved, is to be seen on our stage ; and there is not an effect of which she is not wholly conscious. She can repeat every night, without a hair's-breadth of difference, the apparently spontaneous start, shiver, cry, discord, smile, stagger, gesture or holding back of gesture. Her face is a mirror of the passions, and her voice speaks for each in its own language.

In addition to singing *La Soularde*, *La Grand-Mère* and *Ma Tête*, she gave a series of songs by Baudelaire and Rollinat, set to music by Rollinat. I knew something of Rollinat's work from his rather over-praised book, *Les Névroses*, in which he has tried, much too obviously, to do over again what Baudelaire had done before him with, at all events, the artist's sincerity of perfection in his art. But I had not heard his music, and it interested me, as a poet's music always does, because it is not music at all, but the expression of a poem in sound. Sung as they were, with every gesture of the words visibly audible, in the voice, these songs seemed to me to have a strange, illegitimate beauty of their own. It was like a child crooning to itself, without knowing what it is saying. The splendid and ghastly sonnet of Baudelaire, *La Causerie*, which begins so curiously :

Vous êtes un beau ciel d'automne, clair et rose,

and ends with the despairing cry :

> Calcine les lambeaux qui ont épargné les bêtes !

was certainly never meant to be set to music, never
meant to be sung ; but this setting in which the music
wanders round the words like a bee skimming around
a flower, and their meaning, in which every word had
its own expression quite apart, from the expression of
the music, gave one not less certainly the charm of a
new interpretation to the familiar poem.   To *Les Yeux*
of Rollinat, Yvette succeeded in giving an unwilling
beauty with intensity of expression, and beauty of vocal
intonation with that almost surgical cutting open of
the living flesh of words, which is, after all, her gift.   In
these songs she has her own material over again, common material, which others have left common, but
which she transforms by her use of it, into an art
wholly distinguished, in which she is supreme.

This world of the Café-Chantant, Lautrec—and no
wonder—loved and hated ; . and, by mere force of hating and loving it, understood it absolutely.   He hated
and loved it, I suppose, as one loves and hates a woman,
for her beauty, for her lies, for her evasions, for her
duplicities, for her passions, as in this sonnet :

> I have outlived my life, and linger on,
> Knowing myself the ghost of one that was.
> Come, kindly death, and let my flesh (being grass)
> Nourish some beast's sad life when I am gone.
> What joy is left in all I look upon ?
> I cannot sin, it wearies me.   Alas !
> I loathe the laggard moments as they pass :
> I tire of all but swift oblivion.
>
> Yet, if all power to taste the dear deceit
> Be not outworn or perished utterly ;
> If it could be, then surely it were sweet—

I go down on my knees and pray ; O God,
Send me some last illusion, ere I be
A clod—perhaps at rest—within a clod.

As for satiety, I am certain Lautrec felt that neither more nor less than most men who have sensitive nerves ; and who get weary—alas ! how weary—of the mere pleasures and necessities of sinning : so absolute a part of our lives, who live as men do, being men, for women ; as women, being women, live for men. I quote these lines of Rossetti's *Jenny* ; for his life, being certainly half abnormal, was given up to four subjects, and passionately : poetry, painting, mediaeval mysticism, and women ; and, with the exception of *The White Ship*, a few of the reflective sonnets, and an occasional lyric such as *Cloud Confines*, woman is the subject of all his poems ; and the same may be said of his pictures.

Jenny, you know that city now.
A child can tell the tale there how
Some things which are not yet enrolled
In market-lists are bought and sold
Even till the early Sunday light,
When Saturday night is market-night
Everywhere, be it dry or wet,
And market-night in the Haymarket.
Our learned London children know,
Poor Jenny, all your pride and woe ;
Have seen your lifted silken skirt
Advertise dainties through the dirt ;
Have seen your coach-wheels splash rebuke
On virtue ; and have learned your look
When wealth and health slipped past, you stare
Along the streets alone, and there,
Round the long park, across the bridge.
The cold lamps at the pavement edge
Wind on together and apart,
A fiery serpent for your heart.

Besides the astonishing designs of H. G. Ibels, in an album consecrated to the Café-Concert—the text and designs were reproduced by *l'Echo de Paris*—these of Lautrec are amazing—and veritably Rabelaisian in their abominable accuracy, their incredible depravations, their exaggerated proportions ; in their malice, their sinister significance. Always Yvette in her intricate poses, caught under sudden reflections of the footlights and of the lights over the stage that change her variable face into other varying aspects—with her irregular profile and inspired eyes, wicked with her Parisian malice ; then Judic, malicious and pernicious ; Abdala, who seems to be doing the *Danse du Ventre*, as one saw her in the French Exhibition ; Esmé Lescot, with her too evident hips ; Mary Hamilton, profound and pagan ; Avril, a dancing butterfly in flight in the hot sunshine ; Paula Brébion, disagreeable and luxurious ; Löie Fuller, the flaming firefly.

As for Lautrec, part of his sinister genius shows itself in a desire for the return of that ancient Venus, not dead, but only hidden for a time in the caves of the Venusberg ; of these old pagan gods still going to and fro on the earth, under all kinds of disguises. Nor would he have forgotten the legend of the execution of Apollo—by the spiritual tribunal—and that on the rack he confessed that he was the God Apollo ; and that, having been suffered to play once more on his lyre and to sing a song, so intense was the magic of it that all the women wept and many of them soon afterwards fell sick and so died and went down into hell. " And "— so Heine says—" some time afterwards the people wished to drag him from the grave again, that a stake might be driven through his body, in the belief he had been a vampire, and that the sick woman would by this means return to life. But they found the grave empty."

Lautrec looks back to that evil age of the Medicis in France, when, during the massacre of Saint Bartholomew's Eve, men's very visions being distorted, their imagination turned into forms of hideous cruelty and in their nostrils the surfeit of blood, when the very gutters ran blood, and when the carnal and cruel and insane King Charles fired neither the first nor the last shot in that carnage : when poisoned perfumes swung in the heated air like incense out of censers ; when delirium had thunder on its wings ; when Coligny lay suffering in the fiery August atmosphere from the shot of an ambiguous assassin, before the Duke de Guise " sets the sickle in the corn " and has the Admiral slain ; then it is that Charles, exotic and over-nervous, with on him always the horrible desire of the scent of blood, precipitates the event,—this king who had always hunted as a madman,—driven now finally by his own delirium on the scent of human blood.

XXII

LAUTREC's life and his art are indissoluble. Out of his tragic existence he created what no painter could have conceived and created whose existence had not been one prolonged tragedy. He had not the vision of Manet or of Degas. To Manet, in his vision of the world, everything existed in hard outline ; in seeing and in rendering what he saw he has, above all, audacity, he cannot conceal his delight in the paint which comes out of his brush like life itself. Turn to

Lautrec: notice one of his portraits, which anticipates some of the after-effects of colour, and gazes into our eyes with a triumphant sensuality of soul, implacable, interrogatory. Turn from this to some of the portraits of Degas ; he always does what he wants, his pictures have the beauty of consummate skill, they have all that ingenuity of mind and mastery of line can give us ; they are miraculous pieces of drawing, which every artist must admire, as he would admire a drawing of Leonardo, but then they end where the Leonardo drawing does but begin.

Lautrec was the painter of depraved souls in depraved bodies. In his vision of the unseen he is comparable with certain painters of greater genius. The direct representation of anything unseen to the eye, and only mediately conceived by the imagination, can only affect us in the way intended by the artist if it makes its appeal to us by its qualities of beautiful lines, beautiful colour or beauty of composition. Blake, at his best, is so tremendous because, in his endeavours to give form to the morning stars singing together, and God riding on the whirlwind, and the worms talking to one another on the earth, he creates line, and the movement of figures—and the passion of gesture, with so unwearied an energy. When the line is wrong, I wrote, the conception dwindles ; no profound meaning was ever conveyed in pictural form except through sureness of hand, through a technique definitely excellent in its own way. This might be applied to certain details in many of Lautrec's pictures and in those of Guys. The mistake—as I have often said—of those who have praised such a painter as Blake for his conception, and condemned him for his tech-

nique, lies in a confusion between what is artistically
right, that is, truthful to beauty, and what is academically correct, that is, faithful to rule. God's arm in the
drawing of the beginning of *Europe* is out of all human
proportions, in a figure done after the ordinary type of
humanity ; but the arm is technically superb, because
it expresses the instant energy of omnipotence, not to
the mind, but to the mind through the eye, unhesi-
tatingly. In any case, whatever has been said for and
against him, Lautrec is supremely great. " Et, pour
la première fois, peut-être, un peintre porteur d'un
nom à panache, avec un entrain non feint, ira vers
les plus crapuleux spectacles, pour les exprimer, non
pas, comme on l'a cru, avec une férocite de nain
haineux, mais avec une verve passionnée, avec une
tenace ivresse, avec un don de tout son génie."

In *Certains* of Huysmans there is a study of Bianchi's
Virgin and Saints in the Louvre, a picture which seems
to have interested him solely because, as he says, " de
cette toile s'exhalent pour moi des emanations délicieuses, des captations dolentes, d'insidieux sacrilèges,
des prières troubles." The same odour of corruption
emanates from I know not how many of Lautrec's
paintings. This is the vision of Huysmans of " that
sweet creature of the double sexes," the Hermaphrodite :

" Ce ne sont pas plus les yeux navrés, les yeux purs,
les yeux de source, limpides et froides, du saint Benoît,
ce sont des yeux brûlés par des tentations qui abouti-
rent. Et l'aspect du saint fait rêver. Ces formes de
garçonne, aux hanches un peu développées, ce col de
fille, aux chairs blanches ainsi qu'une moelle de
surceau, cette bouche aux lèvres spoliatrices, cette
taille élancée, ces doigts fureteurs égarés sur une arms,

ce renflement de la cuirasse, qui bombe à la place des seins et protège la chute divulguée du buste, ce linge qui s'aperçoit sous l'aisselle demeurée libre entre l'epaulière et le gorgerin, même ce ruban blue de petite fille, attaché sous le menton, obsédent. Toutes les assimilations éperdues de Sodome paraissent avoir été concenties par cet androgyne dont l'insinuante beauté, maintenant endolorie, se révèle purifiée déjà, comme transfigurée par la lente approche d'un Dieu."

I am certain that this perverse and adorable picture was one of those that most persistently haunted Lautrec's vision : those subtle incarnations of evil, those suggestions of the mystery of the flesh, its inexplicable suggestiveness to the sensations and the senses, the incense swung in some invisible senses ; and, mixed in this lurid air with metallic refractions, might not some element of mockery be inextricably mingled ?

XXIII

" WHAT malady is comparable with that of alcohol ? " These words Edgar Poe wrote, some time before he was found, drugged and stupefied, in one of the rum shops used for voting, then taken to the hospital, where he expired, in an alarming delirium. His nerves created his genius, and therefore only nervous writers have understood him. By his caprices, his fantastic follies, his exasperations, his natural insolence, his passionate excitations, his bitter satire, his fashion of annihilating deserved and undeserved reputations ; by the fact that he had not enough grip in his constitution to live wisely ; that his evil star inevitably doomed him to a tragic death ; by what are called his delinquencies in regard to morals ; for such propensities as these he has been generally misunderstood.

In Lautrec's case, there were delinquencies enough in all conscience, certainly not against morals as they are usually understood—or (as I have said) misunderstood : but absolute, but to him fatal and most necessary, but to him part of his overwhelming temperament, but to him part of his admitted abnormality. He had used, indeed abused, too many spirituous liquors : he had taken too little care to preserve, on another side, that body of his that had served him, so far, prodigiously.   It was not through excess of drink, it was through excess of living, in a word it was through all his excesses, that he let himself be ruined.

Baudelaire in his *Notes on Poe* in which he reveals Poe's genius and defects in as irrefutable a fashion as that of the Sphinx without an Enigma, refers to a unknown power, *un penchant primordial*, which makes inexplicable the actions—good and evil—of men of genius.   This primitive, irresistible force is that form of perversity which makes man ceaselessly homicidal and suicidal, assassin and hangman ; for, it has been said with a remarkably satanical subtlety, the impossibility of finding a sufficient motive for certain evil and perilous actions might lead us to consider them as the result of the Devil's suggestions, if experience and history had not taught us, that God often derives from these the establishment of order and the chastisement of criminals : *après s'être servi des mêmes coquins comme des complices ! tel est le mot qui se glisse, je l'avoue, dans mon esprit, comme un sousentendu aussi perfide qu'-inevitable.*

Perversity ! the most sublime and the most sinister

word that exists, is, for one thing, *un penchant primordial*, and, for another, " the primal need," and, for another, men's greed after women, women's greed after men ; it exists in violent animal peace and in the stirrings of the blood ; in all the sexual instincts ; in all the appetites ; in the imagination and in the creator's nerves. I do not admit for one instant that there was an equal perversity in Poe and in Lautrec : for, as I have said, the elements of their perversity were elementally unlike. And, for my part (without disguising what has always been in me a peculiar kind of perversity), neither man nor woman, book nor picture, scent nor savour, that has none of this quality, can give me the fascination I require. Can one imagine a Dusé, a Lautrec, a Rodin, a John, a Pachmann—to name five of the greatest artists I have known, all with their different kinds of genius—without Perversity ?

In 1899 Lautrec's eccentricities become so notorious that most people suppose him to be absolutely mad, He is not exactly that, in spite of the insanity in his veins ; he is more than ever the prey of his hallucinations, in which there are long intervals of lucidity ; in the meanwhile he has been sent to the house of Dr. Samalque at Saint James. I find from a letter written to me by Ernest Dowson, Hôtel de St. Malo, Paris, March 7th, 1899, the exact date in regard to Lautrec's entrance into Saint James : " I am intrigued by your card. It is from a serious Belgian consulate or a jest from Dublin ? If it is the former, I can only imagine that Leopold has discovered my merit and decided on decorating me. Toulouse-Lautrec, you will be sorry to hear, was taken to a lunatic asylum yesterday."

Il y a de quoi devenir fou, Lautrec certainly said to

himself, after his reason had returned to him, quoting
the words of Gérard de Nerval ; having also awakened
out of a dream, perhaps refracted from some broken,
illuminating angle by which madness catches unseen
light, revealing to him the meaning of his own super-
stition, fatality, malady. It might have occurred to
Lautrec to wonder what really can be the link which
holds our faculties together ; being so intensely conscious of his nerves' illusions, of their disillusions, of
their imaginative discords. Yet Lautrec always dis-
tinguishes the causes of certain of his moods from
those other causes which come to him because he is an
artist, and are properly concerned with that creation
which is his own function. Did the obscure and fatal
irritation of his madness reveal to him visions he had
never seen before, visions of worlds unrealized, Hamlet's disembodied visions ? To have been obstinate
in depravity, as Lautrec was ; to have remembered
this sentence, "when, with mental malignity, he
persuades men that the works of the Holy Spirit are
the works of the Devil," to have had the sensation of a
world in which the daylight has been abolished, when
men stumble in a perpetual night ; to have wondered
if he had ever been in the emotional state of the man
in *Adolphe* : *Je me reposais, pour ainsi dire, dans
l'indifferences des autres, de la fatigue de son amour*,
that marvellous phrase which has in it so much of the
intolerable indifference of love's fatigue and of passion's
satieties, of the intolerable indifference a man of genius
is bound to have toward a woman who is intolerable ;
to have chased some divine shadow, through one hot
day and to return tired and to find the visitor just
turning away from the closed door—and for that to

be an obsession ; to have felt a subtle terror growing out of the waters, with a more ghastly insistence than anything solid on the earth ; finally, to have had the shock on his nerves which came to him as he read this sentence in *Sur Cathérine de Médicis* of Balzac, speaking of the Calvinist martyr who is recovering after having been tortured : *On ne saurait croire à quel point un homme, seul dans son lit et malade, devient personnel* :— all this is exactly what I imagine Lautrec must have felt during the last two years of his tragic life.

The great artist, Toulouse-Lautrec, had no more illusions. There was no more for him any Rubes-querat, who created myriads of illusions, a scornful and a cruel Queen, wily and unwise, who finally—as finally Lautrec is bound to—loses her own illusions, and is no more their mistress ; all that is left for her is mischief. Yet, before then, as such wicked adven-turesses did to Lautrec, her power remains her own.

" So she clenched her hands an instant," writes Meredith, " with that feeling which knocketh a nail in the coffin of a desire not dead, and controlled herself, and went to the youth, breaking into beams of beauty ; and an enchanting sumptuousness breathed round her, so that in spite of himself Shibli Bagarag suffered her to take him by the hand and lead him from that orchard through the shivered door, and into the palace and the hall of the jasper pillars. Strange thrills went up his arms from the touch of the Queen, and they were as little snakes twisting and darting up, biting poison bites of irritating blissfulness."

What now is left, since death knocks at the very gates of his life, for Lautrec ? No more irritating poison-bites from women's lips, no more Liliths to seduce

him, no more dead desires. Nothing, nothing at all ;
only for him to jest over his own condition with a
disconcerting cynicism and a cold-blooded irony.

A certain sinister event, of which Lautrec is either
the direct or the indirect cause, gives him—in the few
years that remain to him, much of the " fever called
Living " that burns in one's brain ; much of " the
terrible torture of thirst," of the fancy (I quote Poe's
poem, *For Annie*) that anyone might start at " beholding him dead," of the thought that the " crisis," this
serious crisis that has come on him, might prove fatal
—an actual repugnance to Paris. For, knowing him
lost (such news flies fast in Paris) certain of those who
had met him at La Nouvelle Athènes, and certain
dealers—known to all artists as swindlers, arrant thieves,
and dishonourable liars—pounced on him ; and in so
abominable a manner, that their atrocity reminds me
of the Furies who pursued Orestes and Clytemnestra ;
only, the Furies were rightly named Ministers of Vengeance.

" And while he falleth," says one of the Furies in
the *Eumenides* of Aeschylus, " yet doth a man know it
not, from the disease of folly ; so thick is the gloom
in which pollution hovers over him ; a cloud of darkness
hanging as it were above his house becomes the
theme of many a sighing tale. For it abideth. Able
are we to contrive and to effect, and with long memories
for evil, awful ones and inexorable to men, adminis-
tering a chosen province though rejected with dishonour
by the gods above and separated from them by the
sunless mould."

It was none of these, whose abiding place is below
the earth and in the sun-forsaken gloom, who attacked

Lautrec ; but, in a literal sense, those who had no sense of honour, no sense of pity, no sense of mercy, as the actual Furies had. With fingers for talons, those miserable creatures thrust into the still nervous fingers of Lautrec, as he sat in some café, the mere material for him to trace designs on.

Painting being his *métier*, Lautrec had but little spare time for reading, finding novels simply stupid ; but, apart from that, he was the most pernicious and malicious diviner of the human comedy that ever existed : he saw always the comic, he saw always the tragic, side of things ; and he was much too inhuman ever to disguise the storms and tempests that he endured, in his imagination, and bodily. So—as hatred of isolation grew on him—he would never let you go, by day or by night, when he was in need of you. In a certain sense he was like Rossetti : the slave of his own imagination, and how little command he had over that or over his genius is painfully enough known. So, having no more feeling for nature as nature than Rossetti had, he never had from nature any consolation, any soothing of any of his sorrows, even the deepest of all—the sorrow of sorrows, Sin.

That Lautrec was capable of deeper depths of sinning than any of his contemporaries—more so, really, than Verlaine, in spite of the immense difference between them—is a lamentable fact, which can only be explained by the madness he certainly inherited. There is not one picture of his that does not show traces of insanity ; by a deformation, an exaggeration, by an infernal craft : always these traces remain. Nor did any artist of our time choose so deliberate, so inevitably fatal, a way of ruining his own existence. It was in his blood, it was in his genius. Yet never, on any occasion, did he, like Dowson, become under the influence of wine almost literally insane, and quite irresponsible ; only, at times, he fell into unreasoning and furious passions ; a vocabulary before then unknown to him, sprang up like a whirlwind ; he seemed always about to commit some act of absurd violence.

I have written :

" For, there is not a dream which may not come true, if we have the energy which makes, or chooses, our own fate. We can always, in this world, get what we want, if we will it intensely and persistently enough. Whether we shall get it sooner or later is the concern of fate ; but we shall get it. It may come when we have no longer any use for it, when we have gone on willing it out of habit, so as not to confess that we might have failed. But it will come."

Lautrec, who had the Devil's energy, did not choose his own fate, any more than Satan ; for (as an Irishman told me on one of the Aran Islands) Satan, being led by pride to equal himself with God, looked into the glass in which only God should look, and when Satan looked into the glass, " Hell was made in a minute." It requires a strong spirit to " sin strongly " and to make one's own profit out of it. Lautrec sinned tremendously, nor did he ever repent of the sins he had committed ; at his own expense he had fallen into " the waste of shame." He contrived to get out of his tragic life almost all he wanted, he got almost all he willed—with an amazing intensity. His was no soul " unspotted from the world " in a body which one sees visibly soiling under one's eyes ; in him, hidden and yet inherent in him, I saw all the fever and turmoil and the unattained dreams of a life which had so much of the swift, disastrous, and suicidal energy of genius.

The Château de Malromé is a beautiful old castle, with towers and turrets, in the department of La Gironde, where Lautrec generally spent part of the summer with his mother.

" I shall always remember," wrote Gustave Coquiot, " this fact. Lautrec was going to leave Paris, and Carabin had met him, in La Place Blanche, before his actual departure for Brittany, when I came on them. Lautrec jeered—jeered abominably. I have never again found for a friend a more agonizing moment. What he had become ! Cowardly, I took Carabin's arm, and we went away. We had from him only one word, brutal. And we knew that this was the end."

Certainly, the end was near at hand ; for no sooner had Lautrec found himself in Tausset, than he was struck by paralysis. His mother, being warned of his condition, came to him, and never left him till he died. He seems (as Baudelaire did before him) to have believed in his cure ; but it is more reasonable to suppose that he forced himself to say so, that he might give some hope to his mother. He died, September 9th, 1901, at the age of thirty-seven.

Certainly, every artist of genius is created to live his life exactly according to his own choice. We get out of life, all of us, what we bring to it ; that, and that only, is what it can teach us. Lautrec was a great creator, by instinct and by imagination, and by an astonishing, a prodigious, mastery of his *métier—Il fut uniquement préoccupé de mettre, comme il disait, les choses à point, d'apprendre son métier, et aussi, et surtout, de vivre la vie qui lui plaisait.* He, in a different sense

from Balzac, dealt in flesh and blood, and knew that
the passions in nature can teach more to the philosopher, and can justify the artist more fully, than all the
unacting intelligence in the world. Both, I am certain,
sought the soul that lurks in some occult corner of our
body ; and that, most of all, it is the soul as nervous
fluid, the executive soul, not the contemplative soul,
that, with rare exceptions, they seek. Both had vision ;
neither, I think, were contemplative. They could surprise the motive force of life, *la recherche d'absolu* ;
and could ask the unanswerable question : " Can man
by thinking find out God ? " Or life, they might
have added ; and then might have answered the
unanswerable question with the great " Perhaps ! " of
Montaigne and the last utterances of Rabelais : " I am
going to leap into the dark. Let down the curtain :
the Farce is over." Still, in regard to Lautrec, it is
worth quoting this sentence of Peter Motteaux on
Rabelais : " We ought not easily to believe, that he,
who even in the most licentious places of his many
companions, is thought by the judicious to have generally a design to expose villainy ; we ought not, I say,
to believe, that such a man, in his seventieth year,
could have abandoned himself to those excesses."

Lautrec's existence, if not disordered—as in certain
senses it was—was ardent, indefatigable, unslackening,
animal, ferocious, insatiable. He—as many other
artists have done—divided his days and nights into
two divisions : one for pleasure, and one for work.
I have never known anyone, with the exception of
Verlaine, who loved the pleasures and the satisfactions
of the flesh so abnormally as he did ; only, with
Verlaine, his genius was often lazy and inactive. This

disorderly life, year after year, the inordinate fatigues that came over him too often, did not, until the end came, succeed in harming or in hurting his astonishing force of physical existence. His failure, his tragical failure was, that he did not give himself enough sleep. Utterly vain is such an one's idea that, with such lack of sleep as he endured, he can go on year after year without ruining his body. He was, one is aware, not normal ; he was, as he himself was vividly aware, abnormal ; as he was born, animal to the last degree of animality, voluptuous and full-blooded, so had he to exist. Cruel, he was capable of kindness, even of ardent affections ; in fact, he found some of his gaiety when he plunged deepest into the sombre waters of Lethe ; as Meredith did in these lines of *Modern Love :*

> But there's a strength to help the desperate weak.
> That night he learnt how silence best can speak
> The awful things when Pity pleads for Sin.
> About the middle of the night her call
> Was heard. And he came wondering to her bed.
> " Now, kiss me, dear ! It may be now ! " she said.
> Lethe had passed those lips, and he knew all.

And, as André Rivoire says : *L'art n'a rien perdu à cette existence effrenée. Toujours et partout, l'artiste y suivait l'homme, et autour de lui cherchait de la beauté. C'est pour avoir su découvrir cette beauté, où personne avant lui ne l'avait si bien découverte qu' Henri de Toulouse-Lautrec restera comme l'un des artistes les plus puissants et les plus originaux de notre époque.*

Did Lautrec, I wonder, when he felt the approach of death, day by day and night by night, when he was sleepless, think of certain declarations of the Catholic Church : *Absorba est mors in victoria. Ubi est, mors,*

victoria tua?   Ubi est, mors, stimulus tuas?   He might
have given up all that consolation, as if any such
consolations were to him then more than hopeless, all
the time his miserable and racked body was longing for
its pain to be over and craving for peace when peace
was not, imagining if there were any chance of the
Spirit surviving the infamy of the grave ; as he saw
in vision, or visibly, he who had lived a life few men
have ever lived, who had longed so passionately for
length of life, and who knew, just then, that length of
life was denied him—the Thing—Death's figure,
hooded and masked and menacing, with all hell's fire
in his cruel lips.   If Lautrec could have turned his
eyes away from the hideous aspect of that Thing—
that Thing that has neither name nor lineage—could
have closed them and turned his face to the wall—
the naked wall that shuts that outer world from our
vision—that might have been wonderful ; only, instead
of being wonderful, the imagination would come over
him of himself utterly dead, the narrow boards of the
coffin waiting—how ignobly !—for his body to be nailed
inside of it ; and then, all the grave's infamy ! And then,
finally, to have fallen asleep, and to have passed for
ever into the common air unfelt by others ; and then, in
Pater's words, " to have experienced the last curiosity."

Had he but read them, Lautrec might have found
his destiny revealed in two lines of Hood—that found
an echo in Baudelaire :

> Anywhere, anywhere
> Out of the world !

For this saying has passed through interpreters, and
helped to make a rare corner of modern literature ; and

the pity of the whole thing is like that of a great line of
Dante, not less universal. Or rather, let this be Lautrec's
epitaph : A stone is flung angrily and straight into the air,
and may strike the canopy before it falls back on the
earth : or, by preference : *Un homme qui improvisait avec
une aprêté terrible et un comique sinistre, ces charges amères
où perçait déjà le dégoût du monde et des ridicules humains.*

THE epithet *fin de siècle* has been given, somewhat loosely, to a great deal of modern French
art, and to art which, in one way or another,
seems to attach itself to contemporary names. Out
of the great art of Manet, the serious art of Degas,
the exquisite art of Whistler, all, in such different
ways, so modern, there has come into existence a new,
very far from great or serious or really exquisite kind
of art, which has expressed itself largely in the *Courrier
Français*, the *Gil Blas Illustré*, and the posters. It
comes into competition with the music halls ; half
contemptuously, it popularizes itself. It finds its own
in the eighteenth century, so that Willette becomes a
kind of witty Watteau of Montmartre ; it juggles with
iron bars and masses of shadow, like Lautrec. And,
in its direct assault on the nerves, it pushes naughtiness
to obscenity, degrades observation into caricature, dexterity of line and handling being cultivated as one
cultivates a particular, deadly *botte* in fencing.

And this art, this art of the day and hour, competes
not merely with the appeal and the popularity of the
theatrical spectator, but directly with theatrical methods,
the methods of stage illusion. The art of the ballet
counts for much ; in the evolution of many favourite
effects of contemporary drawing, and not merely
because Degas has drawn dancers, with his reserved,

essentially classical mastery of form. By its rapidity
of flight within bounds, by its bird-like and flower-
like caprice of colour and motion, by that appeal to the
imagination which comes from its silence (to which
music is but like an accompanying shadow, so closely,
so discreetly, does it follow the feet of the dancers),
by its appeal to the eyes and to the senses, its adorable
artificiality, the ballet has tempted almost every
draughtsman, as the interiors of music-halls have also
been singularly tempting, with their extraordinary
tricks of light, their suddenness of gesture, their
triumphant tinsel, their fantastic humanity. And
pantomime, too, in the French and correct, rather than
in the English and incorrect, sense of the word, has
had its significant influence. In those pathetic gaieties
of Willette, in the windy laughter of the frivolities of
Chéret, it is the masquerades, the English clown or
acrobat seen at the Folies-Bergère, painted people
mimicking puppets, who have begotten this masquer-
ading humanity of posters and illustrated papers.
And the point of view is the point of view of Pierrot—

> le subtil génie
> De sa malice infinie
> De poète-grimacier—
> —Verlaine's *Pierrot Gamin.*

In Rodin's drawings there is little of the delicacy of
beauty. And here, it would seem (if indeed accident
did not enter so largely into the matter) that a point
in sentiment had been reached in which the perverse
idealism of Baudelaire has disappeared, and a simpler
kind of cynicism takes its place. In these astonishing
drawings from the nude we see woman carried to a

farther point of simplicity than even in Degas : woman
the animal ; woman, in a strange sense, the idol.
Not even the Japanese have simplified drawing to this
illuminating scrawl of four lines, enclosing the whole
mystery of the flesh.

Degas, also, has done something that neither the
painter nor the draughtsman of Europe has ever done.
He studies nature under the paint by which woman,
after all, makes herself more woman ; the ensign of
her trade, her flag as the enemy. He gets the nature
of this artificial thing,—that the Japanese had in a
sense invented—and the skin underneath it, and the
soul under the skin. Watteau and the Court painters
have given us the dainty exterior charm of the masquerade, woman when she plays at being woman,
among " lyres and flutes." Degas has done much
more than this, with other elements in his pure design.
The drawing of Degas, setting itself new tasks, exercises
its technique upon shapeless bodies in tubs, and the
strained muscles of the dancer's leg as she does " side-
practice." What he has not done, and others in our
time have done, is taking all the ugliness of sex disguising itself for its own ends : that new nature which
vice and custom make out of the honest curves and
colours of natural things.

Yet Degas, with all his genius and his cunning
instinct for contrasted colours and pure outlines and
luxurious attitudes and marvellous mastery of design,
has never achieved such drawings as certain of Rodin's ;
for instance, as one where a woman faces you, her legs
thrown above her head ; as, for instance, one where
she faces you with legs thrust out before her, the soles
of her feet seem close and gigantic. She squats like

a toad, she stretches herself like a cat, she stands rigid, she lies abandoned.

When Gustave Moreau is at his best (as when the cactus, his favourite flower, becomes a marvel of rosy flame : when he tries to make the leaves mysterious, not by painting them as they are, but in softening what is sharply artificial and unreal in the actual thing), when his colour is almost a disguise, and the conventional drawing, the doll-like figures, the forced emphasis, the prettinesses, are buried out of sight under clots of paint, out of which the sunlight sucks a fiercer brilliance, there are moments when it is possible to compare him with Degas, the painter of modern things, whose work is to be seen in the Louvre and in the Luxembourg. What Moreau does with colour combined with outside reality, Degas does—and more discreetly, with colour caught in real things : a hanging on a wall, a carpet under the feet, a frame of theatrical scenery, which becomes a vision as he looks at it, and the equivalent of imagination. And in Degas the beauty is a part of truth, a beauty which our eyes are too jaded to distinguish in the things around us.

I find a curious coincidence in the word I have used, " jaded," in these sentences that Pater wrote on *Le Byron de nos Jours* of Browning :

" In this poem we have a single moment of passion thrown into relief in this exquisite way. Those two jaded Parisians are not intrinsically interesting ; they only begin to interest us, when thrown into a choice situation. But to discriminate that moment to make it appreciable by us, that we may find it, what a cobweb of allusions, what doubt and treble reflections of the mind upon itself, what an artificial light is constructed and broken over the chosen situation ; on how fine a needle's point that little world of passion is balanced ! Yet, in spite of this intricacy, the poem has the clear ring of a central motive ; we received from it the impression of one imaginative soul, of a single creative art."

Degas, then, finds in real things, seen at the right moment, all the flames and all the jewels of Moreau. And thus, in his acceptance of reality, he has created a new and vital form of art, while Moreau in his rejection of time and space, has but combined pictures out of other pictures. His art was sterile from the first, and but repeats the ineffectual spells of a solitary magician. But at least he lived his own life, among his chosen spectres.

It has been said that beauty can only be rendered by fine technique, but that beauty can be found in technique only. Degas is typical of the school to which subject-matter is indifferent, treatment everything. Or it would be more correct to say that the uglier the subject, the better excuse does it give for virtuosity of technique ; so that Degas in his revolt against the academic treatment of the nude, pretty under impossible conditions, strips a middle-aged model, sets her to stand in a tin bath and squeeze a sponge over her shoulders, so that the attitude reveals every thickening crease of flesh, every falling away of contour, every physical degradation of age, the very impress of the whalebones of the corset, the line which darkens, the neck where the collar of the dress had ended. Painting the dancer, he takes us behind the scenes, showing us two homely girls in practising-dress, straining a leg forward and backward, while the shoulder-blades stand out like knives, and the whole body aches with effort. And Degas does what he wants, his pictures have the beauty of consummate skill, they have all that ingenuity of mind and mastery of line can give us ; they are miraculous pieces of drawing, which every artist must admire, as he would admire a drawing by Leonardo ; but there they end, where the Leonardo drawing does but begin.

Again, where Velasquez accepts life, making it distinguished by his way of seeing it, not so much choosing from among its moments as compelling a moment to give up the secret of a lifetime ; where Whistler gives us the ghost of the river, people who are the phantasms of moods and moments, a whole shadowy world, in which beauty trembles and flutters, and is a breath escaping upon a sigh ; so when Degas paints one of his finest pictures, *L'Absinthe*, done perhaps in the same manner as *Le Bon Rock* of Manet, he gives one, in his more modern way, an equal vision of reality. The man is Desboutins, a Bohemian painter, in a mood of grim dissatisfaction, who is just as living as the depraved woman who sits beside him— before the glass of absinthe that shines like an enormous and sea-green jewel—with eyes in which much of her shameful existence is betrayed, without pity, without malice.

These are not mysterious like Whistler's creations, in whose pictures the mystery is for the most part indefinable. They are unlike his fashionable women who draw on their gloves in the simplest of daily attitudes ; unlike his portraits of children, who stand in the middle of the floor to be looked at ; unlike his men in black coats who are thinking thoughts which

DEGAS
L'Absinthe

they hide from us. Degas' two people have the vividness of hallucination. And how far from the dull insistence of ordinary life, from the unmeaning or deceiving mask which most people present to the world, are these actual and uncommon people whom he has dreamed on canvas, and they are there !

In Manet there is nothing but good painting. Look at a girl's head, and you will find in it a magic which is not magic at all, as far as magic is an evasion or a message from outside nature : the life that is there is a life of frank paint, neither asserting nor correcting itself ; there is no sentiment which we can be conscious of, no tenderness as with Carrière, yet still less is there the scientific coldness of Cézanne. It is as if the painters were like the sun itself ; an energy beyond good and evil, an immense benevolence, creating without choice or preference out of the need of giving birth to light. There never was such homage to light, to light as the principle of life as *Le Linge*, where the vivifying rays of that impartial sunlight can soak with equal thirst into the ugliness of the child and into the loveliness of the linen. And you may hate the picture as you may hate a day of overpowering heat, yet be no more able to get away from it than you could withdraw from the ardour of nature.

For, to Manet, in his vision of the world, everything existed in hard outline. In seeing, and in rendering what he saw, Manet has, above all, audacity ; he cannot conceal his delight in the paint which comes out of his brush like life itself. Think of his *Olympia*, which in one room of the Luxembourg deadens and empties of life every picture hung near it, as Whistler's *Portrait of his Mother* does in the next room.

Never, as Watteau, " a seeker after something in
the world, that is there in no satisfying measure or not
at all," Degas, implacable *farouche*, the inexorable
observer of women's flesh, in the wings of music-
halls, in café-concerts, loves and hates and adores this
strange mystery of women's flesh, which he evokes,
often curiously poisonous, but always with a caressing
touch, a magic atmosphere that gives heat and life and
light to all his pictures. Where Renoir is pagan and
sensual, Degas is sensuous and a moralist. In the
purity of his science, the perhaps impurity of his
passion, he is inimitable. Is not his style—for painters
have their own styles—the style of sensation—a style
which is almost entirely made of sensations? He
flashes on our vision *la vrai vérité* of things, the very
essence of them—not so much the essence of truth as
of what appears in the visible world, of the visible
world to the eyes that see it. And—if I may invent
an image—he " coners " the soul of inner things
outwardly realized.

Colours have their passions like lovers. In Degas
they flame and burn and turn furious and amorous.
In his pastels the flesh lives more vividly than in any
modern painter ; that is to say, in his peculiar and
particular method of painting, in which he is as
astonishingly original as Manet. No one ever painted
maquillage as he does, nor the strokes of light that shine
on a dancer's eyes, nor the silk of her rose-coloured
tights that outline her nervous legs ; nor the effects
—sudden and certain—of what I have seen for years
from the stage : silhouettes and faces and bodies and
patches of light, a cigarette in a man's mouth ; and,
in the wings, miracles of change, of caprice, of fantasy,

of what seems and is not an endless motion of the
dancers. I do not for one moment imagine that there
is one secret—however secret that might be to most
observers—that he has not observed, caught and
rendered, with that sudden instinct that guides one's
imagination.

I am one of those who have shared his passion for
those adorable creatures ; created, one supposes, for
the pleasure of appealing to our senses and for the
pleasures that they give and take.

> Intoxicatingly
> Her eyes across the footlights gleam
> (The wine of love, the wine of dream)
> Her eyes, that gleam for me !
> And O, intoxicatingly,
> When, at the moment's close,
> She dies into the rapture of repose,
> Her eyes, that gleam for me !

I have always felt that the rhythm of dancing is a
kind of arrested music ; as Degas has certainly often
done : as in the feet that poise, the silent waves of
wandering sound of her body's melody, and her magic.
He gives ravishing beauty in his *Danseuses se baissant*
when he catches the exquisite instant as they bend,
legs crossed, the right hand placed lightly on the floor
of the stage, the left one in almost one straight line
from the shoulder ; giving to both the same gestures,
the same (what one has so often seen) half slipping
off of the corsage from the stooping shoulders, and,
with the indication of their thin arms, their favourite
decorations : the bracelet round the wrist, the necklace
round the throat that flies out in the mere wind of their
arrested attitude.

Degas sees no demons in the air nor malice in every bush and bough as Lautrec did ; nor does he see passion as the infamy of our hearts, a shameless and perilous thing that strips naked the body of life. Yet, I think I am right in saying that he did see all these things, as in *La Chanteuse Verte*, where a hideous woman bows to the audience, in a red dress, with vulgar gestures ; she has sung an obscene song ; she has not what is called *le trac* ; but, as she interrogates her public, knows that they must respond to her desires, she, who flatters all the vices. And again when a brazen creature opens her mouth wide, like a vampire, if one can imagine a vampire in a café-concert, dressed abominably and wearing flowers, certainly the sensation he gives is marvellous ; for beyond her gleam the orange rosy lights of Les Ambassadeurs and below her one sees glimpses of vague Parisian heads. And in one of his astounding paintings of a night café there is a crudity of colour, a brutal vigour, with a kind of hatred of these prostitutes, ugly and hideously alive, whose faces fill the spaces between white pillars, as the noises of the Boulevard dwindle into an ominous silence. And this is where " l'artiste paraît avoir été attiré par l'aspect canaille et lamentable à la fois de certaines types de filles."

The painter of modern life, Degas has the genius of the Parisians ; not that he paints Paris, but that he always paints in Paris ; and so for him, as for Balzac and Baudelaire, the choice of what one chooses in Paris has a new savour, like scented wine. Dancing-girls, washerwomen in the laundries and those exquisite young girls one sees every dawn in Paris carrying

DEGAS
The Dancer with the Bouquet

linen, singers in café-concerts, jockeys, naked women,
women in baths, in dressing-rooms and in shops, in
the stalls and in the boxes with their men : these are
his chief delights,—the inconceivable delights of one
of so fine a temperament, of such sensitive nerves, of
such experienced eyes, whose vision's intensity is
haunted by human faces in movement, always with a
sense of movement on even what is arrested, in the
factitious light of gas, in fact in all forms of shades and
lights that this magician in paint has revealed to us.

From the first one required a certain initiation in
order to understand his surprising originality, his
dazzling audacity, his absolute sincerity to that form
of art that he created. Exactly the same occurred in
the cases of Delacroix and of Baudelaire. It is impossible not to see the influence of that great painter in
Degas ; not only in their marriages and adulteries of
colours. "The design of creation is the privilege of
the man of genius," wrote Baudelaire, profoundly.
Both, like nature, had a horror of the void. Both
give the sensation of what such imaginations can
create—not as the genius of Goya created monsters
and devils and witches and depraved monks and
Satanical Sabbats—but the finite in the infinite ;
visions produced by prodigious conceptions, "Car-
tooned " as it were, beforehand, by a process intensely
conscious, patient and silent. In Delacroix's pictures
are eagle-headed creatures contemplating the sun,
serpent women coiled with serpents ; and, in what is
symbolical in Degas' pictures, there are curious
analogies with these. "Comme tous ceux de mon
âge," said Delacroix to Baudelaire, in words Degas
might have used, "j'ai connu plusieurs passions ;

mais ce n'est que dans le travail que je me suis parfaitement heureux."

Take, for instance, this pastel. One sees a box that gives on the stage, with the rose-red colour of a half-lifted screen, showing the sombre purple of the ceiling ; a woman's profile leans over from the balcony above the box as she gazes on the singers as they shout ; the line of her cheeks is heightened by the heat of the hall, the blood rises in her cheek-bones, whose sanguine colour, as ardent as in the ears, fades away on her forehead. Compare certain dashes of strong colours on this pastel with what one sees in the *Massacre de Scio* of Delacroix : a Greek or Turkish sachet painted in the foreground, knotted with white knots, crude and brutal in their extremes of tonality. Suppose you efface this sachet, the harmony of the picture would be destroyed.

Degas sees in woman all that is irresponsible for good and evil, all that is unreliable in her brain and will, all that is alluring in her variability. He sees women vividly disturbing men's lives—now a modern Circe, now a modern Thaïs. He sees more than that : he sees what these women neither see nor know ; not even what their dreams might reveal to them ; not even what their lovers imagine they know of their mistresses. He is never impartial ; he never judges them. He takes them as they are—as perhaps no painter ever did—lets them know that he takes them as they are, that he treats them as they are ; and then alone with them in his studio, he disposes of them as he likes : but, always, he paints. And the rest to him is more or less indifferent. He shows their animality with a kind of ironical disdain—not that of the man of the world ; but with the cruelty of a creator of Images of Good and Evil. A man of singular, but not of universal genius, he seems to have chosen deliberately, I do not say his limits—for he has none, in a literal sense—but such limits as gave him entire scope for the revelation of exactly what his genius, in Blake's phrase, " dictated to him." And so, his work being done, Degas leaves a sense of intense regret behind him ; having created a new art in painting : that is to say, in painting the Sex he adored, without pity and without malice.

CONSTANTIN GUYS

THE history of the Grands Boulevards in Paris has never yet been written. They live on the pages of Balzac, of Flaubert, of Cladel, of Mendès ; they live in the creations of Gavarni and Daumier and Constantin Guys. In writing of Guys, Baudelaire says :

" Some people have justly compared the works of Gavarni and of Daumier with *La Comédie Humaine*, as being commentaries on his novels. Balzac himself, I am convinced, would not have hesitated in adopting this idea, which is just in the sense that the genius of the artistic painter of morals is that of a mixed genius ; that is to say that there enters into it a good deal of the literary imagination."

Always, the Boulevards have an odd and an extraordinary fascination for those who love Paris most at the hour when dusk comes on, stealthy as the silent feet of night, more exciting than any hour in the day ; the hour of *apéritifs* and the hours that follow them till long after midnight. " *Sur la terrasse, entre la rangée de fiacres et le vitrage, une pelouse de femmes, une floraison de chignons échappés du crayon de Guys, attifées de toilettes invraisemblables, se prélassaient sur les chaises ; les unes conservaient sur leurs genoux un gros bouquet, les autres un petit chien, les autres rien.*" There certainly, in the little ironical masterpieces, *Les*

Demoiselles de Bienfilâtre, is Villiers's exasperated vision of the Boulevard des Italiens in 1883.

The Guys to whom Villiers refers is Constantin Guys, who was born December 3rd, 1805, and who died at the age of eighty-seven and was one of the most original and paradoxical artists of his time. *Le Peintre de la Vie Moderne* (1863) of Baudelaire, written on him, is tremendously amusing, cynical, subtle ; and there is much in it of the writer's personality, together with that taste and spirit of modernity which existed in Guys and in Baudelaire. Both adored the old, odd, squalid and sordid and brilliant streets that went for so much in one's days and nights in Paris. Night comes, and Guys wanders from the Latin Quarter to the Boulevard ; it is the *bizarre* and dubious hour when the sky's curtains are closed and the street-lamps are lighted. He follows the light as one follows one's own shadow, where the city's life swarms at its intensest heat ; where the passions in men's and women's eyes and in their speaking mouths are drawn into him by a kind of magnetism ; where the most exquisite creature is seen, driven in her carriage in the middle of the street, turning her eyes in a languid indifference on a woman who has come from the lowest depths, and who scowls at her.

What Guys seeks with most passion is modernity ; for on the Boulevard one sees every form of modernity in what is transitory, fugitive, eternally immobile. He seizes the dramatic moments, and as he draws them, exaggerates them. His imagination is so vivid that he can create furiously original drawings as he studies the dim lights behind the stages of music-halls, and the glaring lights along the Boulevard Saint-Martin.

Constantin Guys is the historian of the women of his generation ; he is their absolutely accurate historian. There remains much that is hermetically sealed and secret in the adventurous, the wandering, the always insatiably curious existence of Guys ; yet what we know of him, among a hundred different things, is his passionate love of all the forms of life that passed before his (at times) abnormal vision. This observer of all the morals is never in default ; for just as he expresses the allurement of certain women, so he represents, with an exact science, all that visible prostitution which is for the most part made for men's cynical amusement. He renders in a marvellous fashion the subtle movements of the professional women as they leave their houses, their evil houses or the houses where they are supposed to live alone and for no other reason than their inevitable fascination. He wanders with them in the Folies-Bergère, where, in the continual flux and reflux, they push themselves against one simply as animal against animal ; for in these Parisian music-halls there is an immense provocation of the flesh as much so the last time I was in Paris as ever before. I have only to read Baudelaire and Huysmans and the Goncourts, and then to imagine how varied were their sensations, their sense of feminine attractions and repulsions. It is terrible to think how many men of genius have dealt largely with the question of the repulsiveness of women : not only Petronius did so, but the saints of all the centuries as well, and the moralists and the immoralists.

Guys's designs of women are dated by the fashion. The rapidity and the breadth of his composition show how precisely he marks the costume of those wanderers

of the Second Empire who were designated by the
names of *biches* and *cocottes*. They wore large skirts,
crinolines, high-heeled shoes, tightly-drawn white
stockings, a toque on their heads, their heavy tresses
falling on both sides of the ears, the chignon in a hair-
net. Guys takes us with him everywhere ; we are
with him in the streets, in the cafés, in the theatres,
in the dressing-rooms, in the balls, in the brothels,
in the Moulin-Rouge, in the Folies-Bergère. In the
garden of Mabille, for instance, he portrays the women's
avid eyes, exasperating the men's cynical desires ; both
sexes equally wary and observant and—what can I
call it ?

> Wine, the red coals, the flaring gas,
> Bring out a brighter tone in cheeks
> That learn at home before the glass
> The flush that eloquently speaks.
>
> The blue-grey smoke of cigarettes
> Curls from the lessening ends that glow ;
> The men are thinking of the bets,
> The women of the debts they owe.
>
> Then their eyes meet, and in their eyes
> The accustomed smile comes up to call,
> A look half-miserably wise,
> Half-heedlessly ironical.

Here, for instance, are two women : this one does
not talk, she waits near two men who are talking ; the
other, occupied in the conquest of two men, images
with her *macabre* profile, her lamentable air, the unconsciousness of passivity. Again he shows a box in
a theatre, with rather fabricated people in it : it is
what one sees of the stage that counts. A café-concert
singer in evening dress holds herself in front of the

corbeille of other women seated in a circle, her arms gesticulating, her mouth wide open. The dancing girls, in the petals of their skirts, are grouped like the flowers in a bouquet ; Thérésa, dressed in black *décolletée* in a long slit, a black collar round her neck, shows the historical portrait of a great artist before her audience. Then he shows professional dancing girls, who rejoice in their rhythmical steps, in the sound of the music to which they dance ; one dressed in blue, with rouge on her cheeks, a rose in the lace of her bodice, is holding her heavy skirt and shows her stockings and shoes. Another, standing apart, whose little head is hooded, shows her white skirts, her tiny feet in tinier shoes ; one sees her tremble, the moment before she joins the crowd.

All that is feverish and delirious in these balls is felt intensely by Guys. He has noted the fury of the *chahut*, in two women back to back, who lift their legs and show the double reflection of their varnished shoes and of their calves before they do the *grand écart*; and in two others, who, with aspects and attractions even more devilish, turn half-naked, with one leg held in one hand. One, a malicious and vicious type, throws her skirt over her shoulders : and before her, as always, is the avid group of admiring men.

What is dominant in this incomparable painter of prostitution, beyond all discussion of technical execution, is expression ; and it is infinitely profound and vehement, sanguinary as the after-sunset I see in the sky to-night, tenebrous in its purple magnificence, a Goya after-sunset. He is always on the watch to seize upon and portray the inner self of these living apparitions ; as in one instance where he shows a woman of the popular type, magnificently dressed, her breasts rigid, her long eyes, lengthened by artifice, avowing their duplicity. The artist's execution aids in creating this expression, not only by the daintiness of the outlines, but by the sensuous mouth, the curved nose, the laughing eyes, and by the vibration that one divines in the figure under the farthingale, made by tintings rapidly washed in with the brush.

In a Spanish scene appears one of the most extraordinary Oriental designs that Guys ever made. The whole composition is one ferocious festival, whirled onward by the winds of all the desires, crowned by half-naked girls who wave their fans as their mantillas shake, showing their nervous legs and the coloured skirts that seem to live an excited life of their own. Two lovely Spanish women are lolling backward in a carriage ; they have wicked eyes, their black hair is held in by combs ; their expression is of passion, piquancy. A fair creature rides behind a matador on horseback, her dress slipping off her white shoulders. The composition is delirious ; all this cavalcade traverses the page like a whirlwind, and one veritably believes that it will disappear before one's eyes, leaving the page blank.

We touch the bottom of the Parisian sewer in the scenes of prostitution drawn by Guys. He groups in the corner of a street three women, two young and one old ; the young ones wear hats, they are dressed in shawls that show their small waists. Again he shows two mere silhouettes, standing against the vision of a narrow lane, the obscurity troubled by the fire of some gas-lamps. He enters the Evil Houses ; he sees women seated on divans. Six women seated

GUYS

Sketch at the Moulin-Rouge

in a room direct their eyes in the direction of the door ; they are breathless, they indicate by their attitudes that someone is entering. He enters, the gentleman without whom these cannot exist ; and the instant after he has entered their room he is their equal.

This does not prevent him from assuming an air of ridiculous superiority : the man who professes his contempt for the women he has come to enjoy. One sees him stand, hat on head, hands in pockets, balancing himself in a dandified fashion, as he leans against the divan where some of the women are seated. He and they know he has his choice of this infamous flower-garden ; some are eager, some utterly indifferent : they and he know that, having chosen his night-companion, he goes ·with her, arm in arm, lifting the hangings.

The observation of Guys is spontaneous, vivid and vital ; he can represent scenes that are morbid, morose, mad, real, fantastic. He fixes on his loose sheets of paper an extraordinary twilight, where gas-lamps shine as in those rooms of Evil Houses they are reflected in the hectic skin of faces, of shoulders and arms. In the mystery of these closed chambers, with low ceilings, with floors and walls arranged so as to conceal all noise, with heavy hangings, where the silhouettes are shadowy and rapid, one is plunged into a hideously heated nightmare out of which surge strange sensations, animal faces ; men dressed in black, women dressed in sombre costumes, who seem to be sorceresses, demons, beasts of the night such as one sees in the paintings of those who have portrayed the temptation which St. Antony endured in the seventh circle of hell.

HONORÉ DAUMIER

HONORÉ DAUMIER was born at Marseilles on February 26th, 1808; he died at Valmondois on February 11th, 1879. Charles Philipon, who created in *La Caricature* the distinct type of the modern illustrated satirical journal, employed on his staff Daumier, Monnier, Traviès, Pigal, and many others. Baudelaire, who had before him the whole series, wrote : " C'est un tohu-bohu, un capharnaüm, une prodigieuse comédie satanique, tantôt bouffonne, tantôt sanglante, où defilent affublées de costumes variés et grotesques, toutes les honorabilités politiques." He added : " Comme artiste, ce qui le distingue, c'est la certitude : il a une mémoire merveilleuse et quasi divine qui lui tient lieu de modèle." Certainly, before Lautrec, he cruelly crucified on imaginary crosses his worst, and his country's, worst enemies. He wielded a scourge. Designing always from memory and from an astonishing intensity of observation, he modelled his designs in wet clay.

In 1860 Gavarni printed one of Daumier's coloured designs, *L'Ivresse de Silène*, which has the Bacchic joy and the sensuality of Rubens ; and there is in it, said Goncourt : " quelque chose de gaulois, de dru et de libre, que l'on ne trouverait peut-être nulle part ailleurs que dans Rabelais." Curiously, Daumier began to paint in 1848 ; till then the finer part of his genius seems to have lain dormant.

131

Rue Transnonain, le 15 *Avril,* 1834, is a masterpiece of horror ; the tumbled bed, the overturned chair, chaos and confusion, the half-naked dead man prostrate on the floor who crushes under his corpse a little child; there is blood everywhere, blood on the woman's corpse. It was just then, after the expiration of *La Caricature,* that Daumier devoted himself almost exclusively to *Le Charivari.* Robert Macaire was originally created by " Frédérick "—Lemaître. Banville tells us how the great actor in the melodrama of *L'Auberge des Adrets,* in this bizarre and bloody buffoonery, presented Robert Macaire in the image of " un forçat moraliste, un dandy en guenilles, un fantoche féroce, charmant et insensé, faisant tenir dans le cadre de la vulgaire tragédie une vaste satire littéraire et politique." Daumier re-created Macaire, a monstrous being, sinister, relentless, an immoral and an immortal type of all the Vices. It is no wonder that Balzac, having seen it, cried : " There's something of Michelangelo in this fellow ! " And that Baudelaire should have written : " Robert Macaire fut l'inauguration décisive de la caricature de mœurs. *La Caricature,* dès lors, prit une allure nouvelle ; et ne fut plus spécialement politique. Elle fut la satire générale des citoyens. Elle entra dans la domaine du roman."

I have been studying, in Barbizon House, one of the finest collections of Daumier's paintings and drawings I have ever seen. One realizes the influence of Delacroix : the effect of his genius on modern pictures and modern painting was immense. In any case, Daumier's work shows a prodigious prodigality of means and of materials, together with a sinister imagination, and an abnormality in which he is in unison with Goya, Hogarth, Breughel, Callot. There is an immense vitality in all his figures, abject or caricatured, deformed or transformed, wonderful, heroic, sordid, tragic, bestial. There is vehemence and violence in his vision, which, when it creates nightmares, spreads a feeling of intense horror over some close and poisonous atmosphere ; as, for instance, in *Watering Horses*, where the half-naked man on the horse seems to surge out of the canvas in, as it were, two embodied gestures. I have rarely seen such a depth of sinister and Satanical invention and meaning as in *Lune de Miel*, which represents, in No-man's-land, two of the strangest lovers that ever existed. One envisages them against an immense hill which mocks them by its inscrutability. To all this they are insensible. Linked together, there is something fearful in their grimaces. Inimitable as ingenious, the vertical top-hat of the man, a Marnette out of Balzac, overtops the hill. One knows Daumier's lifelong hatred of *Avocats* : they writhe, exult, become comic, insolent, hideous, revolting, pitiless ; he makes them triumph. His satire here and everywhere is as biting and lacerating as that of Rabelais and Swift.

Daumier's signed drawing, *La Parade*, of two mountebanks, has that inimitable quality which I find only in Balzac and in Baudelaire : you cannot get away from its terrific and pitiable appeal ; the man with a defiant face who beats the drum, the ghastly clown who stands beside him in a despairing attitude on a chair ; the irony of their destiny has fastened them there—naked enough before the unseen crowd —outside their booth. This effect which I have always seen in Paris, is wrenched out of reality into a reality which has no excess, which is poignant, tragic, primitive.

Cervantes' *Don Quixote* haunted Daumier's imagination : he has the same morbid and masculine vision, the same grim humour. The Knight could not exist without Sancho ; Pantagruel could not exist without Panurge. The types are eternal. Don Quixote annihilates Time and Space, he changes the aspect of the Universe. *Don Quixote and the Windmills* and certain of his other paintings remind me of the Escorial, an example of what the one will can and cannot do ; the divine spark of genius was lacking in Philip's impotent creation, who, a fanatic, built those prison walls about him in this mountainous place of dust and grey granite, in which every line is rigid, every colour ashen, in a kind of stony immobility more terrible than any other images of death.

L'Arrivée au Chemin de Fer is singular and sinister ; startling, it seizes one, in the mere vision of eight people entering the platform, where I see his genius in the elimination of details, in the formidable fixity of these figures, in the massing of them ; in the thick paint, the reds and purples of the women's dresses, the blue scarf that waves in the wind ; in the sharp leaden division between two transparent patches of colour ; one is hatched in with masses of orange yellow : and, again, one sees the influence of Balzac, in whose creations the Finite clashes with the Infinite.

It is an interesting fact that Baudelaire entered into possession of his three rooms under the roof of the Hôtel Pimodan, originally the Hôtel de Lauzun, 17 Quai d'Anjou, in 1843 ; for these luxurious rooms he paid three hundred and fifty francs a year. Daumier lived for the greater part of his life near Baudelaire, before he went to the Hôtel Lambert. Daumier's

DAUMIER

La Parade

genius, to whom Baudelaire, with a flash of wonderful insight, attributes " the strange and astonishing qualities of a great genius, sick of genius," has in it certain elements that have so much horror in them that the sense literally reels, as it were, before an open sewer. His abnormality, together with the pure sanity of his vision, the *homo duplex* which lives within him, combine in creating things one can only wonder at ; such as his huge composition : " Enfoncé Lafayette ! Ventripotent," says Raymond Escholier, " les cuisses lourdes et courtes, bien reconnaisable a ses favoris, a son nez bourbonien, a ses lèvres enfoncées, Louis Philippe, des ses mains jointes, cache une partie de son visage, comme s'il pleurait ; et pourtant, visiblement l'hypocrite s'esclaffe, tout son être exulte, a la pensée délicieuse que l'idole du peuple vient de disparaître." Another of his terrible designs represents a prisoner's last agony, he lies gasping on his deathbed ; Louis Philippe, who holds his pulse, says to the Judge : " Celui-là, on peut le mettre en liberté, il n'est plus dangereux." Like one of Goya's *Caprichos*, it hurts one's very vitals.

Le Haleur is a ghost-like evocation of one of those misty afternoons when the barges crawl past with inexpressible slowness ; coming out slowly after the horse and the rope from under the bridge, with a woman leaning motionless against the helm, and drifting on as if they were not moving at all. Daumier shows you the sluggish river, with banks on both sides ; this, like the canals in London, has a mysterious quality, made up of sordid and beautiful elements, now a dark trail, horrible, crawling secretly.

Au Théâtre is one of his most dramatic and excitingly

Parisian pictures : Hamlet, who has slain Polonius, points with his rapier at Ophelia, who, her hair floating down her back, her hands raised in anguish, tries to escape his vengeance. The whole pit is one uproar, gaping wide-mouthed at these horrors.

Les Voleurs et l'Ane, a night effect worthy of Rembrandt, seizes one by the atrocious representation of the fierce struggle of two men ; one holds the other —who lies on his back, his naked feet in the air— by the throat, as if in the act of strangling him.

Daumier's genius is essentially dramatic ; and, in nearly all of his caricatures, he is singularly original. It has been said of him that his style is grand and elemental, his matter trivial ; his effect is the angry assault of that drawing on this matter, the tilt of the lance against the windmill : in a word, a Cervantes who paints. Turn over his drawings and you will see, in their fantastic and poignant reality, all that Paris contains of living monstrosities ; all that is sinister, cruel, comic, abominable. It is not the Paris of Balzac, it is the Paris of Daumier.

I have never forgotten one of the finest Daumiers I have ever seen : a huge cartoon, unfinished, for his Christ Mocked. It is a shadow, but all is there, all the world in the scrawled heads and backs, and the devil perhaps in the finger of the world's scorn pointed at Christ, a ghost of judgment, who stands and is patient. Here, in this cartoon, is great imaginative work ; to have seen it is to realize something of the gulf which divides imagination (that is, spiritual reality) from fancy (that is, the germ of romance).

JEAN LOUIS FORAIN

" IN more ways than one do men sacrifice to the
rebellious angels," says St. Augustine ; and
Beardsley's sacrifice, together with that of all
great decadent art, the art of Rops, or the art of Baudelaire, is really a sacrifice to the eternal beauty, and only
seemingly to the Powers of Evil. And, in such great
artists, one must see in their verse and painting and
drawing, not only purity of line and of design, of colour
and substance, but the soul that sins, sorrowfully,
without reluctance, inevitably. Beauty we must have :
sin transformed or transfigured by beauty ; abstract
and occult spiritual corruption ; at times the sight of
the feet of the fallen angels, at times a diabolical beauty
revealed in forms of hideousness : beauty divided and
not divided against itself. And in some we want
mockery, human and inhuman, symbolical and tragic,
the obsession of desire denied, beauty's degradation,
masked desires hidden under painted dominoes, that
dance to the sound of the Seven Sins. We want also,
in embodied forms, the signs in the eyes and mouths of
bitter ironies, and what seems to cry out of insatiable
eyes.

Consider, now, the art of Forain. It is an art,
derived first slightly, from Carpeaux, then directly from
Monet and Degas. Yet, in spite of these influences,
his work is always original. Whether he draws or

137

paints, in oils, in water-colours, or in other mediums, he is always startling to one's senses, astonishing to one's sensations. Take, for instance, the captious corruption of a dressing-room in a theatre, the tones of lights and shadows, the spices of the flesh, as in one of his Pastels : and notice the extraordinary difference between this and a painting of a similar interior where the actress sits before her mirror ; we see her begin her make-up ; she tilts her head backward to see the effect of her hair.

Then imagine another, rather in the manner of Degas, where in the wings a tall woman comes forward leaning on a man's arm ; she wears a gorgeous dress and the other man, in evening-dress, moves out of her way ; all, obviously enough, aware of her professional smile. And the whole canvas lives, with disordered life ; one feels it and one sees it.

Degas has painted the fascination of women's flesh supremely. Forain paints the Folies-Bergère ; translates the whole horror and atrocity of the thing into a kind of carnival ; shows the scene, the audience, the bars, the men and women, the sense of movement, of the heated atmosphere, of the very smoke of cigarettes. And, again in the wings, the little painted dancers on tiptoe as they talk to a Balzacian Hulot who grimaces at them ; one seizes snatches of their conversation, catches their gestures ; one sees others gazing on them with envious eyes, or half-seen turning to one laughing faces. He can be cruel to them, satirize them, after the fashion of a splendid draughtsman who might once have been an eighteenth-century *abbé*.

Baudelaire was more learned, more perverse, more deliberate in his visualizing the Vices than Forain.

The latter's technique is complicated. He has made extraordinary water-colours heightened with touches of oil, scenes in café-concerts and in brothels and in the bars of music-halls. He gives one the sharp savourous scent of colours studiously spiced ; and obtains, as he unites unimaginable effects, shades of a curious exactness, by the absolute science of an imaginative Alchemist.

So he paints women *as* women : this one with alluring eyes, with her cold and ambiguous smile, the glorious masses of her hair soaked in strange mixtures ; with some of Lautrec's effects, where some tinge of green finds its way invariably into flesh-colour ; where one sees something green in rouged cheeks, in peroxide-of-hydrogen hair. But he never uses an aniline dye, poisoning nature, as Lautrec did ; who, being tempted by tenebrous spirits, set himself to paint a green shadow on faces, on those of the people who sit night after night outside the cafés in Montmartre.

I have before me one of his finest etchings : *Le quart d'heure de Rabelais*. It represents a private room in a restaurant, seen just before the man and woman are preparing to leave. In the red-papered room one sees a divan ; the man—a big fat ugly creature—is being helped into his overcoat by an uglier waiter, while the woman puts on her bonnet before the glass, scribbled over with names ; exactly as in Rossetti's *Jenny*, when the man sees her reflection—

> Where teems with first foreshadowings
> Your pier-glass scrawled with diamond rings.

And one sees, in the sordid aspect of this particular place, how the hired woman carelessly arranges her hair, as if she had totally forgotten the existence of the man who never looks at her ; he, apparently stifled by the heat, looks at nothing, as he is tortured by the pulls and tugs of the—as one says in argot—*Larbin*.

Forain alone gives one the concentrated quintessence of all that passes on the boulevards in Paris, and of the interiors of cafés and of private rooms. Yet has not everyone who has lived in Paris noticed, in daylight, the banality of these rooms where one lives only at night, when all that is faded takes the peculiar tones of lights and shadow, with all the luxury and intoxication that one finds in Paris and in Paris only ? *Le Café de la Nouvelle Athènes* is superb—a vision of reality caught by I know not what inspiration. There is the angle, the tables, the glasses, the bottles, the match-boxes ; there sit two men in top-hats reading newspapers ; top-hats are hung—as they always are —from pegs on the wall ; there stands the hideous waiter in conversation with a *cocotte*, thin-waisted and perverse.

Le Bal des Folies-Bergère is curiously different from Manet's. One sees the circular tables, the people seated, the living crowd that seems to move and that does not move ; and a most singular view of the staircase up which vague figures ascend. The centre is a Manet-like *cocotte*, fashionable, who holds her fan in her hand : one sees her black chignon, her smart bonnet ; and she talks, of course, with an odious *gommeux* whose fixed stare does not even disconcert her.

One, *Le Cabinet particulier*, is magnificent in conception as in execution. It represents a room where the table shows that the three have dined : as in the

wine-glasses, the coffee ; and one girl in chemise with
bare arms sits on the edge of the table ; black curled
hair falls across her face, as the other who leans her
head on her hand, elbow on table, leans forward.
Hideous, bald-headed, bearded, an old Jew sits
crouched on the end of the divan ; he seems to try to
read *Le Soir*. In the whole thing there is fine irony ;
and, as in another picture where a naked woman lies
abandoned on a bed like a coiled snake, here also is
sheer mastery of genius.

It is certainly strange that Forain should, in the
midst of his usual work, have devoted himself to doing
etchings on religious subjects : yet, to me, one or two
of these might be compared—at whatever distance—
with those done by the greatest masters. Take, for
instance, not only *Le Calvaire* (1902), so utterly perfect
in execution that, even in its poignant modernity, it
brings before one's vision the actual Golgotha, but *Le
Retour de l'Enfant prodigue*, in which I find an almost
unspeakable sense of rapture in the passionate tenacity
of the embrace of father and son ; they have rushed
into each other's arms, as the heat of the noon bears
witness. This, indeed, might almost be compared
with a Rembrandt, who has been wrongly accused of
sensationalism in his use of light, of sacrificing truth to
effect. At times he seems to do so, but he cannot dis-
tribute his light with the indifference of the painter to
whom all visible things are equally important. He
takes sides with people and things (does not Forain
also ?), loves and hates them (does not Forain also ?),
and light is his touchstone, it draws and dissolves,
creates and criticizes.

Perhaps it were better, on the whole, to compare

Forain with Rubens. Forain's creations are never evoked by tenderness ; nor are they ever made to look beautiful because they have inherited beauty by right of birth. Where he is most like Rubens is in his content with the appearance and mere energy of life ; and, if anything, more content than Rubens, in the joy of merely being and moving which captures the senses. But, his taste for flesh being simply Parisian, he never attains for an instant Rubens' inexhaustible hunger and thirst for the flesh. To Forain, to most of his curious creations, satiety is almost everything : to Rubens satiety is unknown.

HENRY DE GROUX is a Belgian of Breton origin, the son of a painter, Charles de Groux, whose work is to be seen in many of the picture-galleries of Belgium. In 1892, at about the age of twenty-five, he had a considerable success in Paris, when his immense picture, *Le Christ aux Outrages*, was sent from Brussels at the expense of King Leopold II, and exhibited, first in a sort of shed in the rue Alain-Chartier, and afterwards in the Salon des Art-Liberaux. Other pictures followed, and were seen under better conditions ; a new painter, of disconcerting originality, seemed to have appeared ; in 1899 a special number of *La Plume* was devoted to " *L'Œuvre de Henry de Groux*," containing articles by Camille Lemonnier, Charles Morice, Léon Bloy, Octave Mirbeau, and many others, and nearly a hundred reproductions of pictures, drawings and lithographs. Then, gradually, the interest died down, the new painter was succeeded by other new painters, and in France and Belgium Henry de Groux is now hardly more than a name ; his pictures are buried in the depths of I know not what vague and unfriendly *garde-meubles*, and he himself is living obscurely in Florence, where I saw him dragging vast canvases about a bare studio in which there was nothing but vast canvases and a grand piano.

Imagine a large and naked face, with long and scanty blond hair straggling across a high forehead ; a profile devoured by an exorbitant nose, from which the chin retreats ; the mouth of an orator, the cheeks of an actor, the eyes of a stealthy dreamer ; a manner of ecclesiastical unction, broken through by abrupt nerves and an irony whose ferocity seems to turn inward upon itself ; and imagine this paradoxical being, enveloped to the heels in a red plush dressing-gown, cut after some feminine fashion, staggering at one side of a picture twice his height, while the beautiful woman whose face he has so often painted, never making it quite as beautiful as it is, staggered at the other side of the picture, in a perilous, continual shifting from end to end of the studio.

And imagine all the while a flood of talk, a torrent of ideas, sensations, confessions ; vehement and sensitive criticism of pictures, books and music, a sane intellectual wit, together with a feverish and irrational comment of personal impulses. Outside the pages of Balzac, I have never met so complete an incarnation of a type which only Balzac could create : the type of the eager, inflexible, pitiless, exultant and defeated man of genius, sacrificing everything for an idea, drunk with the desire of creation, with the desire of glory ; a somnambulist in life, through which he passes with an unconsciousness only rarely struck awake by some obstacle, over which he falls with angry helplessness.

The whole work of de Groux is an attempt to render hallucinations, and he is haunted at once by colours, by gestures, by sounds and by ideas. He has himself described fantastically his " demoniacal " love of colour. " The mere sight," he tells us, " of a freshly prepared palette troubles me and contracts my throat, as it happens with hysterical patients whom the hallucination or the attraction of some misdeed, of some monstrous sacrilege, literally intoxicates ! " Form he sees rather as gesture than as outline ; he sees the energy of movement long before he has distinguished the contours of the thing which moves. But colour is like a literal possession of the devil ; he sees it as flame, as flood, as a storm let loose on the world, or a deluge overwhelming it. There is a kind of cruelty in his lust for colour, and he can never bring it to the point at which he would have it burn, or freeze, or become splendour in destruction. But, above all, he would have it cry aloud, he would hear it in a visible rhythm, as some hear music ; and in the spirals and waves and curved onset of his pointing hands and leaping flames and multitudinous carnages and processions in defeat, I seem to discern a rhythm like that of Wagner's music, or a rhythm which would do in painting what Wagner has done in music. And, lastly, he is haunted by ideas, ideas of a queer subtlety, a fanatical casuistry.

He has painted many martyrdoms, exalting many heroes ; he sees the same surging crowd of the world, an ocean of abysmal filth, churned up against the same rock. Now it is Christ, His human body shapeless with suffering, like a torn rag in the wind of the world's fury ; now it is Savonarola, who has burnt the vanities in Florence, that are to be fuel about his own stake ; now it is Napoleon, who turns his horse backward in retreat, over snow and blood and his last ambition ; now, on a scarcely less apocalyptic canvas, it is Zola hooted by the crowd as he comes out of the Palais de Justice. He has seen " The Bad Shepherds," the evil

" Vintages," " The Grave-digger of the Living " ; he has followed death on obscure ways, where men hang themselves from trees or die under bloody knives ; of him, as of Delacroix, Baudelaire might have said :

> Delacroix, lac de sang, hanté des mauvais anges,
> Ombragé par un bois de sapins toujours vert.

Above all, he has painted fire, the devastation, whether it burns Savonarola or the vanities ; and it is in the painting of fire that he has brought his colour to its highest point of intensity. There is always some suggestion of flame in his pictures, flame turned to rubies and sapphires, as in *The Vision of Beatrice*, or glowing in hair and glittering in jewels, as in the somewhat Rossetti-like portrait of the woman seated in the chair, with the book in her hand. Only Blake has put a more joyous and vehement and poisonous life into flame, and there is something in his painting of flame that actually reminds me of Blake, whose painted work he has never seen.

It is of Blake, naturally, that one thinks before certain canvases and before certain lithographs of de Groux ; and one thinks, also, of El Greco and of his groups of lean and tortured figures, consumed by flames of the soul. De Groux sees in less definite form than either, and with a more cerebral excitement. He paints with a kind of rage, in which his brush seems at times to go headlong, making hieroglyphics of form and spots and stains of colour. He would suggest in paint without the limitation, as it seems to him, of statement ; and when the powerful suggestion, as in *Orestes Pursued by the Furies*, concentrates into a statement so definite as the figure of Athena, the form itself is not always convincing. Yet, in that picture, with its hot and venomous colour, its swirl of evil things that hesitate to be human, its horror as of a nightmare, its almost insane energy, is there not a translation into colour and gesture, into pictorial rhythm of an imagined mood, a mood of unearthly hatred?

It is moods, the witchcraft of the brain, that de Groux paints in these strange, impressive pictures; in a *King Lear*, for instance, where all the rhetoric of nature itself, winds, rains, and lightnings, is seen and heard clamouring over a " foolish, fond old man," alone, and " not in his perfect mind." He does not find sufficient interest in the painting of merely what might happen, literally : take, for example, his *Néron au Bestiaire*, where the lions which surge up against the barrier are mixed with flames, and have the devouring fury but not the precise lineaments of beasts, and where the cruel faces and threatening hands which rise up behind the emperor are mixed with the claws of harpies and the beaks and eyes of furies. He has painted nothing but visions, and if he paints portraits, Zola, or Baudelaire, some mood of his own mind enters into the portrait and turns the likeness into a symbol.

" *Quel visionnaire aimé de Dieu que mon grand et pauvre Henry de Groux !* " writes Léon Bloy, in that amazing book *Le Mendiant Ingrat*, of the painter in whom his own sombre and angry genius seems to be reflected or re-echoed. " *L'humilité et la magnificence*," he says also, " *voilà ce que je trouve en lui.*" Is de Groux really and in any deep inner sense a mystic ? Has he any share in the splendid and consoling convictions of the apocalyptic pamphleteer ? I do not know. I doubt if what may seem in him like the vision of the mystic is not rather the attraction of the gulf, a formidable and furtive curiosity, drawing him to the edge of many precipices, over which he bends dizzily. He is the watcher of obscure agonies, and finds a dark pleasure in spectacular disasters. Is it pity for humanity which sets his imagination, as with the wings of birds of prey, flying towards battle-fields and conflagrations ? Some obsession, certainly, has always an irresistible hand upon him, and, in his work done at that bidding, lays on the spectator, who is able really to see it, the same irresistible hand.

MOREAU has been chiefly praised for qualities which belong rather to literature than to painting, and much of his work is like the idolatry of a savage drugged with opium. He has brought together the spoils of many altars, heaped mythology on mythology, and wrought out of his head a barbarous mosaic of decorative detail, which has been seen in no light in which human eyes ever saw. Legendary figures pose academically among landscapes of vegetable jewels. But in some of his work, done for enamelling or for the tapestry of the Gobelins, fantasies in which plain colour is placed against plain colour, and the drawing is rigid and as if petrified, weave admirable patterns, exactly suiting those two formal mediums. And, in some small water-colours hung in the Luxembourg, among more ambitious failures, there were miracles of sheer painter's colour, hardly attached to anything, a mosaic of precious stones, but with all the inner fires of the jewels flaming out of the canvas.

One, the unluckiest, of these dreamers who have made a world *à rebours*, and have lived persistently in it, " though the world," the other world, may have had only " a horror of their joy," is Simeon Solomon, a painter who lived on, forgotten somewhere or other, until 1905, when his death in the workhouse opened to him once more the doors of the Royal Academy. Had circumstances been kinder to him, or had he been other than himself, he would have been a formidable rival for Burne-Jones, where travellers of his tribe will still be waylaid on the confines of glamour and sleep. Look through the catalogue of the Royal Academy and of the Dudley Gallery, between 1865 and 1872, and you will find picture after picture, from the *Lady in the Chinese Dress*, with its bad drawing and queer, orchid-like colour, and exotic and enigmatical expressiveness, to the Academy *Judith and her attendant going to the Assyrian Camp* of 1872. The very names, *Love in Winter*, *Sacramentum Amoris*, *Hosanna*, suggest Burne-Jones, though they are exactly parallel in date, and are as likely to represent an influence as a following. Others have a more definitely Jewish character, *The Three Holy Children in the Fiery Furnace*, the *Patriarch of the Eastern Church pronouncing the Benediction of Peace*, the *Carrying the Law in the Synagogue of Geneva* ; while perhaps what was most significant in this strange temperament is seen in such pictures as *The Sleepers and the One that Waketh*. Three faces, faint with languor, two with closed eyes and the other with eyes wearily open, lean together, cheek on cheek, between white, sharp-edged stars in a background of dim sky. These faces, with their spectral pallor, the robes of faint purple tinged with violet, are full of morbid delicacy, like the painting of a perfume. Here, as always, there is weakness, insecurity, but also a very personal sense of beauty, which this only half-mastered technique is just able to bring out upon the canvas, in at least a suggestion of everything that the painter meant.

In later years Solomon restricted himself to single heads drawn in coloured chalks, sometimes two heads facing one another, the Saviour and Mary Magdalen, the Virgin and the Angel of the Annunciation. The drawing becomes more and more nerveless, the expression loses delicacy and hardens into the caricature of an emotion, the faint suggestions of colour become more pronounced, more crudely asserted. In the latest drawings of all, we see no more than the splintering wreck of a painter's technique. But as lately as ten years ago he could still produce, with an almost mechanical ease, sitting at a crowded table in a Clerkenwell news-room, those drawings which we see reproduced by some cheap process of facsimile, in pink or in black, and sold in the picture-shops in Regent Street, Oxford Street, and Museum Street. They have legends under them out of the Bible, in Latin, or out of Dante, in Italian ; or they have the names of the Seven Virtues, or of the Seven Deadly Sins ; or are images of Sleep and Death and Twilight. " A void and wonderfully vague desire " fills all these hollow faces, as water fills the hollow pools of the sand ; they have the sorrow of those who have no cause for sorrow except that they are as they are in a world not made after their pattern. The lips are sucked back and the chin thrust forward in a languor which becomes a mannerism, like the long thin throats, and heavy half-closed eyes and cheeks haggard with fever or exhaustion. The same face, varied a little in mood, scarcely in feature, serves for Christ and the two Marys, for Sleep and for Lust. The lips are scarcely roughened to indicate a man, the throats scarcely lengthened to indicate a woman. These faces are without sex; they have brooded among ghosts of passions till they have become the ghosts of themselves; the energy of virtue or of sin has gone out of them, and they hang in space, dry, rattling, the husks of desire.

CLEARLY marked off from these painters to whom paint has been no more than a difficult, never really loved or accepted, medium for the translation of dreams or ideas into visible form, yet not without some of their desire of the impossible in paint, Monticelli seems to unite several of the tendencies of modern painting, in a contradiction all his own. I confess that he interests me more than many better painters. He tries to do a thing wholly his own, and is led into one of those confusing and interesting attempts to make one form of art do the work of another form of art as well as its own, which are so characteristic of our century, and which appeal, with so much illegitimate charm, to most speculative minds.

To Monticelli colour is a mood ; or is it that he is so much a painter that mood to him is colour ? Faust and Margaret, or a woman feeding chickens, or a vase of flowers on a table, or a conversation in a park, or a cottage interior, it is as much the same to him as one title or another is the same to a musician. The mood of his own soul, or the fiery idea at the heart of these mere reds and greens and yellows : that is his aim, and the form which offers itself to embody that desire is a somewhat unimportant accident to him. But since form is the language in which alone we can express thought or emotion, so as to be understood in any very positive or complete way, it is his error to be inattentive to language, forgetting how little we can express by gesture and the sound of the voice only.

But he himself, doubtless, is content with the arabesque of the intention, with a voluptuous delight in daring harmonies of colour, as a musician might be content to weave dissonances into fantastic progressions, in a kind of very conscious madness, a Sadism of sound. Monticelli's delights are all violent, and, in their really abstract intoxication of the eyes, can be indicated only in terms of lust and cruelty. Beauty, with him, is a kind of torture, as if sensuality were carried to the point of a rejoicing agony. His colour cries out with the pain of an ecstasy greater than it can bear. A weak and neurotic Turner, seeing feverishly what Turner saw steadily in sky and sea, coupled with a Watteau, to whom courtly elegance and the delicate pathos of pleasure had come to be seen tragically, sombrely, vehemently, might perhaps have painted some of these pictures, or at least thought them in such a manner. The painting itself is like the way of seeing, hurried, fierce, prodigal, the paint laid on by the palette-knife in great lumps which stand out of the canvas. Looked at close, some of these pictures seem to be encrusted with uncut jewels, like the walls of the Wenzel Chapel in the Cathedral of Prague. At the proper distance, the colours clash together in that irreconcilable way which Monticelli meant, crude tone against crude tone ; their conflict is the picture.

In writing of Monticelli it is impossible not to use terms of hearing at least as often as terms of sight. All his painting tends towards the effect of music, with almost the same endeavour to escape from the bondage of matter ; which happens, however, to be the painter's proper material, while it is not the musician's. Monticelli is scarcely at all dependent on what he sees, or rather he sees what he likes, and he always likes the same thing. He tries to purify vision to the point of getting disembodied colour. Other painters have tried to give us the spiritual aspect of colour. He seems to paint listening. Confident, doubtless, in the symbolism by which a sound, a colour, or an emotion may be identical, the expression only being different, not the thing expressed, he hears colour upon a fiery orchestra of his own. And some of the formlessness of his painting undoubtedly comes from that singular confidence of his that the emotional expressiveness of music, together with its apparent escape from formal reality, can be transferred without loss to the art of painting.

Does he not, however, forget that music is really the most formal and even fettered of the arts, a kind of divine mathematics in which the figures on the slate begin to sing ? At one end a dry science, at the other an inspired voice, music can express emotion only by its own severely practical method, and is no more the bird-like improvisation which it is often supposed to be than poetry is the instinctive speech of emotion when it has reached the stage of words. On true principles of analogy, music corresponds to a picture in which there is first of all very careful drawing. But that is not the way in which it is seen by theorists like Monticelli, whom we must take as he is : a painter who would make pictures sing, not according to the rules of music, but according to a seductive misinterpretation of them.

The subjects of Monticelli's pictures are excuses,

and the excuse is sometimes almost humorous. He paints a woman feeding chickens, and the incident is only invented to bring a large figure, so over-real as to be almost spectral, against a background of blue-black storm-clouds. He paints a woman washing clothes, and, as one looks at the picture, one sees at first only a background crackling with flames, then a streak of white in the foreground, a river seen for a moment under the shadow of that great light, and then, finally, a woman bending over the water. He paints a nymph, and we see a coarse woman half-naked, seated at the foot of a tree with a dog at her feet. In another picture two dogs meet in a field, and stare curiously and angrily at one another. Sometimes he seizes upon a really picturesque moment, not neglecting its more obviously dramatic possibilities, as in the scene evoked from *Faust*, or the sober and splendid *Adoration of the Magi*, in which the splendour of robes and crowns has not distracted him from the august meaning of the legend. He is fond of figures arrested in the pause of a dance, like the three Algerian women in the shadow of a doorway, or the tambourine dance in the open space of a park ; curiously fond also of little naked children and of dogs. His painting often conveys the effect of tapestry, as in the large *Meeting in the Park*, with its colour as if stitched into the canvas. His world is a kind of queer, bright, sombre fairyland of his own, where fantastic people sing and dance on the grass, and wander beside fountains, and lie under trees, always in happy landscapes which some fierce thought has turned tragic ; the painter being indeed indifferent to more than the gesture of his puppets in solid paint, who make so little pretence to any individual life of

their own. Their faces are for the most part indistin-
guishable ; all the emotion being in the colour of their
dresses, in their gesture, and in the moment's pattern
which they make upon the green grass or against
ancient walls.

And Monticelli has at least this great quality, among
others less great : every touch of his brush expresses
a personal vision, a way of feeling colour, and is a
protest against that vague sort of seeing everything in
general and feeling nothing at all, which is supposed
to be seeing things as they really are. Things as
they really are ! that paradox for fools. For everyone
probably, for the artist certainly, things are as one sees
them ; and if most people seem to see things in very
much the same way, that is only another proof of the
small amount of individuality in the average man, his
deplorable faculty of imitation, his inability not only
to think but to see for himself. Monticelli creates
with his eyes, putting his own symbols frankly in the
place of nature's ; for that, perhaps, is what it means
to see nature in a personal way.

GUSTAVE MOREAU

I

IN two pictures of Chassériau in the Louvre we see the origin of both Gustave Moreau and Puvis de Chavannes. *La Chaste Suzanne* does what Moreau tries to do, with a certain attractive grace ; the conception much more pictorial, the drawing much more sensitive. The colours are a little faint, dry even, but this slender, romantic figure in a romantic landscape makes a picture. In the fresco which hangs beside the Botticellis on the staircase, there is the suggestion of a fine decoration, anticipating Puvis. Both followers went further, each on his own way, than Chassériau, and have eclipsed his fame ; and for the most part those who accept Puvis reject Moreau, and those who exalt Moreau, like Huysmans (to whom he owes the wider part of his reputation), can seem to themselves to have said all when they have said scornfully : " Comparer Puvis et Gustave Moreau, les marier, alors qu'il s'agit de raffinement, les confondre en une botte d'admiration unique, c'est commettre vraiment une des plus obséquieuses hérésies qui se puissent voir." With which it is possible to agree, in a sense not Huysmans'.

The art-criticism of Huysmans is remarkable as literature, and it is Huysmans who was one of the first to fight on behalf of Degas, of Forain, of the impressionists. But, just as he has written a book on the cathedral of Chartres, and Rodin can say of it, " One does not get much benefit by reading it " ; just as he has written of religion without convincing most Catholics that he is really a sincere Catholic ; just as he has written elaborately about plain-song without making it clear that he understands music ; so, in his eloquent and picturesque writing about pictures, it is rarely from the painter's point of view that he approaches them. In the first edition of *Certains* there was an essay on a picture in the Louvre, a *Virgin and Saints* of Bianchi, a picture which seems to have interested him solely because, as he says, " de cette toile s'exhalent pour moi des émanations délicieuses, des captations dolentes, d'insidieux sacrilèges, des prières troubles." In an essay on Félicien Rops, finer as literature than any of the designs about which he writes, he overlooks all that is cold, trivial, and mechanical in this " diabolic " art, in his delight in its homage and learned eulogy of evil. He writes of Odilon Redon as one would hardly be justified in writing of Blake ; and, finally, seems to find in Gustave Moreau the painter of all others best suited to evoke his own eloquence, a painter at last really palpable, a mine of literature, and he has praised his *Salome* with this elaborate splendour :

" A throne, like the high altar of a cathedral, rose beneath innumerable arches springing from columns, thick-set as Roman pillars, enamelled with vari-coloured bricks, set with mosaics, incrusted with lapis lazuli and sardonyx, in a palace like the basilica of an architecture at once Mussulman and Byzantine. In the centre of the tabernacle surmounting the altar, fronted with rows of circular steps, sat the Tetrarch

Herod, the tiara on his head, his legs pressed together, his hands on his knees. His face was yellow, parchment-like, annulated with wrinkles, withered with age ; his long beard floated like a cloud on the jewelled stars that constellated the robe of netted gold across his breast. Around this statue, motionless, frozen in the sacred pose of a Hindu god, perfumes burned, throwing out clouds of vapour, pierced, as by the phosphorescent eyes of animals, by the fire of precious stones set in the sides of the throne ; then the vapour mounted, unrolling itself beneath arches where the blue smoke mingled with the powdered gold of great sunrays, fallen from the domes.

" In the perverse odour of perfumes, in the overheated atmosphere of this church, Salome, her left arm extended in a gesture of command, her bent right arm holding on the level of the face a great lotus, advances slowly to the sound of a guitar, thrummed by a woman who crouches on the floor.

" With collected, solemn, almost august countenance, she begins the lascivious dance that should waken the sleeping senses of the aged Herod ; her breasts undulate, become rigid at the contact of the whirling necklets ; diamonds sparkle on the dead whiteness of her skin, her bracelets, girdles, rings, shoot sparks ; on her triumphal robe, sewn with pearls, flowered with silver, sheeted with gold, the jewelled breast-plate, whose every stitch is a precious stone, bursts into flame, scatters in snakes of fire, swarms on the ivory-toned, tea-rose flesh, like splendid insects with dazzling wings, marbled with carmine, dotted with morning gold, diapered with steel-blue, streaked with peacock-green.

" In the work of Gustave Moreau, conceived on no scriptural data, des Esseintes saw at last the realization of the strange, superhuman Salome that he had dreamed. She was no more the mere dancing-girl

who, with the corrupt torsion of her limbs, tears a cry
of desire from an old man ; who, with her eddying
breasts, her palpitating body, her quivering thighs,
breaks the energy, melts the will, of a king ; she has
become the symbolic deity of indestructible Lust, the
goddess of immortal Hysteria, the accursed Beauty,
chosen among many by the catalepsy that has stiffened
her limbs, that has hardened her muscles ; the monstrous, indifferent, irresponsible, insensible Beast,
poisoning, like Helen of old, all that go near her, all
that look upon her, all that she touches."

In these pages of *A Rebours* the art of Moreau
culminates, achieves itself, passes into literature.

II

GUSTAVE MOREAU is haunted by the image of Salome,
and he paints her a hundred times, always a rigid
flower of evil, always in the midst of sumptuous glooms
or barbaric splendours : a mosque, a cathedral, a
Hindu temple, an architecture of dreams. She is not
a woman, but a gesture, a symbol of delirium ; a fixed
dream transforms itself into cruel and troubling hallucinations of colour ; strange vaults arch over her, dim
and glimmering, pierced by shafts of light, starting into
blood-red splendours, through which she moves robed
in flowers or jewels, with a hieratic lasciviousness. A
sketch (painted, almost carved, on wood) shows her
swathed in savage fripperies, advancing on the tips of
her toes, her feet and ankles tattooed with jewels, holding the lotus in her right hand, her head crowned by a
tiara ; cloths, ribbons, all sorts of coloured streamers,
swing heavily about her, heavy as lead, the image of an

idol. He sees her always with flames, flowers, and blood about her.

And he is haunted by other tragic women : Delilah, Judith, Messalina, Cleopatra, Helen on the walls of Troy ; he sees even Bathsheba tragically. Unachieved as pictures, coming into existence through all manner of borrowings, they remain graven images of the spectral women that haunt the brain of the student. Helen becomes an image of stone or salt, greenish-white against stone pillars and a sky with white stars ; the face blotted out, a spectre seen by the brain with shut eyes. He paints Cleopatra, and you see an explosion of fierce colour, a *décor*, and then, vaguely, a mere attitude, the woman. He paints Francesca da Rimini, and you see an immense room, with a black window at the back, menacing with light ; then, gradually, a red spot huddled in a corner, which is Francesca. It is the theatre of life which interests him, not life, and not nature : an architecture of the brain, an atmosphere called up out of unrealized space.

Moreau is the mathematician of the fantastic, a calculating visionary. In his portrait of himself one sees a sickly dreamer, hesitating before his own dreams. His effects are combined mentally, as by a voluptuary who is without passion. His painting is sexless and yearning, and renders the legends of sex with a kind of impotent allurement. Leda and the swan recur as a motive, but in the rendering of that intense motive there is no more than decorative toying, within landscapes crackling with ineffectual fire. Sometimes colour is sought, sometimes line ; never the kernel and passion of the story. And it is the same with Helen, Bathsheba, Messalina, Eve and the Serpent, and the

eternal Salome ; always the same strengthless perversity, fumbling in vain about the skirts of evil, of
beauty, and of mystery. What he tries to suggest he
has not realized ; what he realizes he has not seen ;
his emotion is never fundamental, but cerebral ; and it
is only when he shuts it wholly within his colour, and
forces his colour for once to obey his emotion (as in
a little *Magdalene on Calvary*, with the three crosses
black against hills corroded out of sunsets), that he is
able to produce a single imaginative effect, that he is
able to please the eye by more than some square or
corner of jewelled surface into which life comes
surreptitiously.

Moreau, I have heard Rodin say, was a man of
science, a great combiner, one of a generation which
was taught to study art in the galleries, and not from
nature. Out of this art life is rigorously excluded.
His figures, prettified from the antique, are uninteresting and express nothing ; interest comes into the
picture from the surroundings, and in the wake of the
title. His landscapes are made of rocks, trees, water,
hills, and chasms, neither drawn nor coloured after
nature, nor composed on any of nature's plans. His
light is neither that of the sun nor of the moon, but a
light imagined in a studio, and fitted into the pattern of
a design. And this world is peopled with remin-
iscences. He does not even choose among schools or
among ages ; but will be Greek or Hindu indifferently,
and with an equal incapacity for reflecting any faithful
image. He seems to look through coloured glasses,
and when I stand before his pictures I am reminded
of those travellers who, when they cross the sea, put
on red spectacles that they may not see the moving

waves as they are, but after some unnatural and uncomforting compromise of their own.

Moreau has this in common with all visionary artists, that he sees in nature only what he brings into it. But is it really vision which he brings, and under what imaginative light has he seen these feeble shapes and arbitrary brilliances ? Are they not laboriously sought out, made to order, in a sense, not even records of a fever or of a delirium (as in the vast and violent canvases of Henry de Groux), but painstaking fantasies, the rendering of moods in which all the excitement has come mechanically, by the mere " will to dream " ?

When Blake fails, it is the failure to translate a thing seen into a visible thing. Moreau's failure is not that of a vision unachieved, but of a plan imperfectly carried out. Geometry breaks down, a bit of the mosaic has been wrongly placed ; patience or skill has given out before the end is reached. When he paints in pattern, as in the Chinese architecture of his *Chimères*, I cannot feel that he really sees in pattern, but that he has worked it out by a kind of dovetailing, square inch by square inch. He says, I will paint Venice in a symbol ; and he sets towers and domes against the sky, and fills the foreground with a nude figure, clay-coloured and with folded wings, lying at full length among inexplicable bushes. He paints a *Fée aux Griffons*, and it is a Bouguereau transposed into the terms of enamel. He takes a subject of Blake, and paints *Christ in the Garden of Olives*, with a similar flame-winged angel in downward flight. But even here the Parisian ideal of prettiness cannot be driven out of his head, nor the Paris art-student's timid correctness out of his hand.

Beauty, to him, is bounded on the one side by prettiness, on the other by the fantastic and the unnatural.
At a touch of nature his whole world of cold excitement
would drop to pieces, scatter into coloured fragments of
broken glass.

The world of Moreau is made of coloured glass and
jewels. His colour is always startling, sometimes
intense ; like his whole work, it aims at effect, and it is
that portion of his work which most often or most
nearly succeeds. He encrusts his canvases with gesso,
with metal, and with glass. In the Palazzo Martinengo
at Brescia there is a quaint picture of *St. George and
the Dragon*, attributed to Giovanni Donato Mont'
Orfano, which is like an anticipation of this part of
Moreau. The armour is of actual steel and iron, the
lance of iron, and pointed with steel ; there are brass
and steel knobs and nails and circlets on the horse's
harness. Thus, in Moreau's *Fleur Mystique* there is a
design built up like Le Puy, with rocks and haloes and
jewelled crowns and tiaras and petals of tin and stems
of coloured glass. But with Moreau nothing is painted
for its own sake, but for the sake of some enigmatical
transformation. He paints a tea-rose, and the flower
petrifies, turns into a jewel. The cactus, which should
be his favourite flower, becomes a menace of rosy
flame ; but he tries to make the leaves mysterious, not
by painting them as they are, and thus loses much,
softening what is sharply artificial and unreal in the
actual thing. He is at his best, nearest to imagination,
when he sees almost nothing but colour, setting mass
to cry against mass. Thus it is only in his small com-
positions, his sketches, that he makes any genuine
appeal as a painter. In the " Grande Salle " of what

was once his house, and is now the " Musée Moreau," he has let in daylight on vast canvases, and that light shows us all that is threadbare in them, their cold frenzies, their gaudy commonness. In the small, bright, sombre things, in the lower rooms, there is the effect, strange, disconcerting, attractive, of a kind of transposition of whole picture-galleries of pictures. All are translated into another language, in which they speak with a fascinating foreign accent.

III

IN one of the rooms of the Musée Moreau there is a copy of Carpaccio's *St. George and the Dragón*, and by its presence there it seems to make criticism easier. By the side of what is youthful and naïve in Carpaccio's realizing imagination, all these laboured inventions seem to drop away into some sick region of No-man's-land, where an art of spectacular illusion sets a tragic ballet, tragic and Parisian, posturing uncertainly across the footlights of picture-frames. A note which I deciphered on the margin of one of the drawings indicates enough of the aim : " Orphée mourant, toute la Nature en pleurs, tous les animaux—les satyrs, les faunes, les centaures, etc., toutes les créatures des poètes—dans des mouvements de désespoir. Nature en deuil." The stealthy snarer is seen setting his traps for attitudes.

It is not in this way, from the outside, that great art, above all great visionary art, is made. There is equal need of " fundamental brain-work " in a picture and in a poem, if either is to be properly imaginative. All Moreau's pictures are illustrations of legend ; it is only rarely, as in the eternal Salome, that they create a new, personal form for legend, and even Salome is for the most part seen meagrely, a costumed doll, to whom Huysmans must add meaning as he adds a rarer colour. At times the painter can produce an effect of actual hallucination, but the effect is superposed upon a purely academic groundwork ; his drawings are all of studied poses, carefully and unsensitively copied ; colour is called in to give heat and singularity to a structure at once cold and commonplace.

When Moreau is at his best, when his colour is almost a disguise, and the conventional drawing, the doll-like figures, the forced emphasis, the prettiness are buried out of sight under clots of paint, out of which the sunlight sucks a fierce brilliance, there are moments when it is possible to compare him with Degas the painter of modern things, whose work is to be seen not far off on the walls of the Luxembourg. What Moreau does with colour combined outside reality, Degas does, and more discreetly, with colour caught in real things : a hanging on the wall, a carpet under the feet, a frame of theatrical scenery, which becomes a vision ·as he looks at it, and the equivalent of imagination. And in Degas the beauty is a part of truth, a beauty which our eyes are too jaded to distinguish in the things about us. Degas finds in real things, seen at the right moment, all the flames and all the jewels of Moreau. And thus, in his acceptance of reality, he has created a new and vital form of art ; while Moreau, in his rejection of time and space, has but combined pictures out of other pictures. His art was sterile from the first, and but repeats the ineffectual spells of a solitary magician. But at least he lived his own life, among his chosen spectres.

ODILON REDON

THE name of Odilon Redon is known to but few people in France, and to still fewer people in England. Artistic Paris has never had time to think of the artist who lives so quietly in her midst, working patiently at the record of his visions, by no means discouraged by lack of appreciation, but probably tired of expecting it. Here and there the finer and more alert instinct of some man who has himself brought new gifts to his art—Huysmans, Mallarmé, Charles Morice, Emile Hennequin—has divined what there is of vision and creation in this strange, grotesque world which surges only half out of chaos—the world of an artist who has seen day and night.

The work of Odilon Redon—his later work, that which is most characteristic of him—consists of a series of lithographic albums, all published since 1880 : *Dans le Rêve, À Edgar Poe, Les Origines, Hommage à Goya, La Tentation de Saint Antoine, À Gustave Flaubert, Pièces Modernes,* and *Les Fleurs de Mal.* Each album contains from six to ten plates in large folio, printed on *beau papier de Chine,* without text, often without title, or with a vague and tantalizing legend, such as *Au réveil, j'aperçus la Déesse de l'Intelligible, au profil sévère et dur.* So, without an attempt to conciliate the average intelligence, without a word of explanation, without a sign of apology for troubling the brains of his countrymen, Odilon Redon has sent out album after album. So little effect have they produced that it has taken ten years to sell twenty-four out of the twenty-five copies of *Dans le Rêve*. " Reste l'exemplaire."

Odilon Redon is a creator of nightmares. His sense for pure beauty is but slight, or rather for normal beauty ; for he begets upon horror and mystery a new and strange kind of beauty, which astonishes, which terrifies, but which is yet, in his finest work, beauty all the same. Often the work is not beautiful at all : it can be hideous, never ineffective. He is a genuine visionary : he paints what he sees, and he sees through a window which looks out upon a night without stars. His imagination voyages in worlds not realized, voyages scarcely conscious of its direction. He sees chaos, which peoples its gulfs before him. The abyss swarms—*toutes sortes d'effroyable bêtes surgissent*—animal and vegetable life, the germs of things, a creation of the uncreated. The world and men become spectral under his gaze, become transformed into symbols, into apparitions, for which he can give no account often enough. *C'est une apparition—voilà tout !* He paints the soul and its dreams, especially its bad dreams. He has dedicated some of his albums to Flaubert, to Poe, to Baudelaire ; but their work is to him scarcely so much as a starting-point. His imagination seizes on a word, a chance phrase, and transforms it into a picture which goes far beyond and away from the author's intention—as in the design which has for legend the casual words of Poe : " L'œil, comme un ballon bizarre, se dirige vers l'infini." We see an actual eye and an actual balloon : the thing is grotesque.

The sensation produced by the work of Odilon Redon is, above all, a sensation of infinitude, of a world beyond the visible. Every picture is a little corner of space, where no eye has ever pierced. Vision succeeds vision, dizzily. A cunning arrangement of lines gives one the sense of something without beginning or end : spiral coils, or floating tresses, which seem to reach out, winding or unwinding for ever. And as all this has to be done by black and white, Redon has come to express more by mere shadow than one could have conceived possible. One gazes into a mass of blackness, out of which something gradually disengages itself, with the slowness of a nightmare pressing closer and closer. And, with all that, a charm, a sentiment of grace, which twines roses in the hair of the vision of Death. The design, *La Mort*, is certainly his masterpiece. The background is dark ; the huge coils which terminate the body are darker than the background, and plunge heavily into space, doubling hugely upon themselves, coils of living smoke : yet the effect of the picture is one of light— a terror which becomes beautiful as it passes into irony. The death's head, the little vague poverty-stricken face, is white, faint, glimmering under the tendrils of hair and roses : tresses of windy roses which stream along and away with an effect of surprising charm, the lines running out in delicate curves, to be lost in the night. And below, separated from the head by a blotch of sheer blackness, one sees a body, a beautiful, slender supple body, glittering with a strange acute whiteness, with a delicate arm raised to the empty

temples of the skull. Below, in its frightful continu-
ation of the fine morbid flesh of the body, the black
column, the huge and heavy coils, which seem endless.
The legend is from Flaubert. Death speaks, saying,
Mon ironie dépasse toutes les autres.

Ammonaria and *Le Sphinx et la Chimère* are from
the same album, which illustrates *Le Tentation de
Saint Antoine*, and are characteristic, though not the
finest, examples of Redon's work. The scene of
Ammonaria is before the temple of Serapis, at Alexandria. It is a Christian martyr whom they are
scourging : she writhes under the blows, in the cruel
sunlight : one feels the anguish of the bent and
tortured figure, suffering visibly. The other design
renders that marvellous dialogue between the Sphinx
and the Chimera. " C'est que je garde mon secret ! "
says the Sphinx. " Je songe et je calcule. . . . Et
mon regarde que rien ne peut dévier, demeure tendu
à travers les choses sur un horizon inaccessible.
Moi," replies the Chimera, " je suis légère et joy-
euse ! " and it is a veritable hilarity that one discovers,
looking at it rightly, in the regard of the strange
creature : a spasm of ironic laughter in the blots of
blackness which are its eyes, in the mouth that one
divines, in the curl and coil of the whole figure. In
the calm gaze and heavy placid pose of the Sphinx,
lines of immeasurable age above its eyes, there is a
crushing force which weighs on one like a great weight,
something external. The power of the Chimera is
of the mind and over souls. Vague, terrible, a
mockery, a menace, it has the vertigo of the gulf in
its eyes, and it draws men toward those " new perfumes, those larger flowers, those unfelt pleasures,"

which are not to be found in the world. In another design the Chimera, spitting fire from its nostrils, light glittering and leaping on wings and tail, turns on itself, distending its jaws in a vast ironic bark : *la chimère aux yeux verts, tournoie, aboie.* More terrible, more wonderful, more disquieting is *Le Diable avec les sept Péchés cardinaux sous ses Ailes.* The design is black upon black, and it is only slowly that a huge and solemn, almost a maternal face, looms out upon one : Satan, placid, monstrous, and winged, who cradles softly the little vague huddled figures of the seven deadly sins, holding them in his large hands, under the shadow of his wings. And there is another Satan, valiantly insurgent against the light that strikes him, a figure of superb power in revolt. Yet another design shows us Pegasus, his beautiful wing broken, a wing that had felt the high skies, falling horribly upon the rocks : all the agony and resistance of the splendid creature seen in the trampling hoofs and heaving sides, and the head caught back by the fall. Again one sees a delicate twilight landscape of trees and birds, a bit of lovely nature, and in it, with the trouble of a vague nightmare, coming there inexplicably, *Le Joueur*, a man who holds on his shoulders an immense cube painfully : the man and the trees seem surprised to see each other. There is another landscape, a primeval forest, vague and disquieting, and a solitary figure, the figure of a man who is half a tree, like some forgotten deity of a lost race : the forest and the man are at one, and hold converse. And there are heads, heads floating in space, growing on stalks, couched on pedestals ; eyeballs, which voyage phantasmally across the night, which emerge out of nests of fungus, which appear, haloed in light, in the space of sky between huge pillars ; there are spectral negroes, there are centaurs, there are gnomes, a Cyclops (with the right accent of terrifying and yet comic reality), embryonic formless little shapes, and, persuasively, the Sciapodes of Flaubert : " La tête le plus bas possible, c'est le secret du bonheur ! Il y doit avoir quelque part," says Flaubert, " des figures primordiales, dont les corps ne sont que les images," and Redon has drawn them, done the impossible. The Chimera glides mystically through the whole series. Death, the irony ; Life, the dream ; Satan, the visible prince of darkness, pass and repass in the eternal dance of apparitions.

AUBREY BEARDSLEY

IT was in the summer of 1895 that I first met Aubrey Beardsley. A publisher had asked me to form and edit a new kind of magazine, which was to appeal to the public equally in its letterpress and its illustrations : need I say that I am defining *The Savoy* ? It was, I admit, to have been something of a rival to *The Yellow Book*, which had by that time ceased to mark a movement, and had come to be little more than a publisher's magazine. I forget exactly when the expulsion of Beardsley from *The Yellow Book* had occurred ; it had been sufficiently recent, at all events, to make Beardsley singularly ready to fall in with my project when I went to him and asked him to devote himself to illustrating my quarterly. He was supposed, just then, to be dying ; and as I entered the room, and saw him lying out on a couch, horribly white, I wondered if I had come too late. He was full of ideas, full of enthusiasm, and I think it was then that he suggested the name *Savoy*, finally adopted after endless changes and uncertainties.

A little later we met again at Dieppe, where for a month I saw him daily. It was at Dieppe that the *Savoy* was really planned, and it was in the café, which Mr. Sickert has so often painted, that I wrote the slightly pettish and defiant " Editorial Note," which made so many enemies for the first number.

175

Dieppe just then was a meeting-place for the younger generation ; some of us spent the whole summer there, lazily but profitably; others came and went. Beardsley at that time imagined himself to be unable to draw anywhere but in London. He made one or two faint attempts, and even prepared a canvas for a picture which was never painted, in the hospital studio in which M. Jacques Blanche painted the admirable portrait reproduced in the frontispiece. But he found many subjects, some of which he afterwards worked out, in the expressive opportunities of the Casino and the beach. He never walked ; I never saw him look at the sea ; but at night he was almost always to be seen watching the gamblers at *petits chevaux*, studying them with a sort of hypnotized attention for that picture of *The Little Horses*, which was never done. He liked the large deserted rooms, at hours when no one was there ; the sense of frivolous things caught at a moment of suspended life, *en déshabillé*. He would glance occasionally, but with more impatience, at the dances, especially the children's dances, in the concert room ; but he rarely missed a concert, and would glide in every afternoon, and sit on the high benches at the side, always carrying his large, gilt-leather portfolio with the magnificent old, red-lined folio paper, which he would often open, to write some lines in pencil. He was at work then, with an almost pathetic tenacity, at his story, never to be finished, *Under the Hill*, a new version, a parody (like Laforgue's parodies, but how unlike them, or anything !) of the story of Venus and Tannhäuser. Most of it was done at these concerts, and in the little, close writing-room where visitors sat writing letters. The fragment published in the first two numbers of *The Savoy* had passed through many stages before it found its way there, and would have passed through more if it had ever been carried further. Tannhäuser, not quite willingly, had put on *abbé's* disguise, and there were other unwilling disguises in those brilliant, disconnected, fantastic pages, in which every sentence was meditated over, written for its own sake, and left to find its way in its own paragraph. It could never have been finished, for it had never really been begun ; but what undoubted, singular, literary ability there is in it all the same !

I think Beardsley would rather have been a great writer than a great artist ; and I remember, on one occasion, when he had to fill up a form of admission to some library to which I was introducing him, his insistence on describing himself as " man of letters." At one time he was going to write an essay on *Les Liaisons Dangereuses*, at another he had planned a book on Rousseau. But his plans for writing changed even more quickly than his plans for doing drawings, and with less profitable results in the meantime. He has left no prose except that fragment of a story ; and in verse only the three pieces published in *The Savoy*. Here, too, he was terribly anxious to excel ; and his patience over a medium so unfamiliar, and hence so difficult, to him as verse, was infinite. We spent two whole days on the grassy ramparts of the old castle at Arques-la-Bataille, near Dieppe ; I working at something or other in one part, he working at *The Three Musicians* in another. The eight stanzas of that amusing piece of verse are really, in their own way, a *tour de force* ; by sheer power of will, by deliberately saying to himself, " I will write a poem," and by working with such strenuous application that at last a certain result, the kind of result he had willed, did really come about, he succeeded in doing what he had certainly no natural aptitude for doing. How far was that more genuine aspect of his genius also an " infinite capacity for taking pains " ?

It was on the balcony of the Hôtel Henri IV at Arques, one of those September evenings, that I had the only quite serious, almost solemn, conversation I ever had with Beardsley.. Not long before we had gone together to visit Alexander Dumas *fils* at Puy, and it was from talking thoughtfully, but entirely, of that Parisian writer, and his touching, in its unreal way so real, *Dame aux Çamélias* (the novel, not the play), which Beardsley admired so much, that we passed into an unexpectedly intimate mood of speculation. Those stars up yonder, whether they were really the imprisoning worlds of other creatures like ourselves ; the strange ways by which the soul might have come and must certainly go ; death, and the future : it was of such things that I found him speaking, for once without mockery. And he told me then a singular dream or vision which he had had when a child, waking up at night in the moonlight and seeing a great crucifix, with a bleeding Christ, falling off the wall, where certainly there was not, and had never been, any crucifix. It is only by remembering that one conversation, that vision, the tone of awe with which he told it, that I can, with a great effort, imagine to myself the Beardsley whom I knew, with his so positive intelligence, his imaginative sight of the very spirit of man as a thing of definite outline, transformed finally into the Beardsley who died in the peace of the last sacraments of the Church, holding the rosary between his fingers.

Anima naturaliter pagana, Aubrey Beardsley ended a long career, at the age of twenty-six, in the arms of the Church. No artist of our time, none certainly whose work has been in black and white, has reached a more universal, or a more contested fame ; none has formed for himself, out of such alien elements, a more personal originality of manner ; none has had so wide an influence on contemporary art. He had the fatal speed of those who are to die young ; that disquieting completeness and extent of knowledge, that absorption of a lifetime in an hour, which we find in those who hasten to have done their work before noon, knowing that they will not see the evening. He seemed to have read everything, and had his preferences as adroitly in order, as wittily in evidence, as almost any man of letters ; indeed, he seemed to know more, and was a sounder critic, of books than of pictures ; with perhaps a deeper feeling for music than for either. His conversation had a peculiar kind of brilliance, different in order but scarcely inferior in quality to that of any other contemporary master of that art ; a salt, whimsical dogmatism, equally full of convinced egoism and of imperturbable keen-sighted-ness. Generally choosing to be paradoxical, and vehement on behalf of any enthusiasm of the mind, he was the dupe of none of his own statements, or indeed of his own enthusiasms, and, really, very coldly impartial. I scarcely except even his own judgment of himself, in spite of his petulant, amusing self-assertion, so full of the childishness of genius. He thought, and was right in thinking, very highly of himself; he admired himself enormously; but his intellect would never allow itself to be deceived even about his own accomplishments.

This clear, unemotional intellect, emotional only in the perhaps highest sense, where emotion almost ceases to be recognizable, in the abstract, for ideas, for lines, left him, with all his interests in life, with all his sociability, of a sort, essentially very lonely.

One of his poses, as people say, one of those things, that is, in which he was most sincere, was his care in outwardly conforming to the conventions which make for elegance and restraint; his necessity of dressing well, of showing no sign of the professional artist. He had a great contempt for, what seemed to inferior craftsmen, inspiration, for what I have elsewhere called the plenary inspiration of first thoughts; and he hated the outward and visible signs of an inward yeastiness and incoherency. It amused him to denounce everything, certainly, which Baudelaire would have denounced; and, along with some mere *gaminerie*, there was a very serious and adequate theory of art at the back of all his destructive criticisms. It was a profound thing which he said to a friend of mine who asked him whether he ever saw visions: " No," he replied, " I do not allow myself to see them except on paper." All his art is in that phrase.

And he attained, to the full, one certainly of his many desires, and that one, perhaps, of which he was most keenly or most continuously conscious : contemporary fame, the fame of a popular singer or a professional beauty, the fame of Yvette Guilbert or of Cléo de Mérode. And there was logic in his insist-

ence on this point, in his eagerness after immediate
and clamorous success. Others might have waited ;
he knew that he had not the time to wait. After all,
posthumous fame is not a very cheering prospect to
look forward to, on the part of those who have worked
without recompense, if the pleasure or the relief of
work is not enough in itself. Every artist has his
own secret, beyond the obvious one, of why he works.
So far as it is not the mere need of earning one's living,
it is generally some unhappiness, some dissatisfaction
with the things about one, some too desperate or too
contemptuous sense of the meaning of existence. At
one period of his life a man works at his art to please
a woman ; then he works because he has not pleased
the woman ; and then because he is tired of pleasing
her. Work for the work's sake it always must be, in
a profound sense ; and with Beardsley, not less
certainly than with Blake or with Rossetti. But that
other, that accidental, insidious, significant motive,
was, with Beardsley, the desire to fill his few working
years with the immediate echo of a great notoriety.

Pierrot is one of the types of our century, of the
moment in which we live, or of the moment, perhaps,
out of which we are just passing. Pierrot is passionate ;
but he does not believe in great passions. He feels
himself to be sickening with a fever, or else perilously
convalescent ; for love is a disease, which he is too
weak to resist or endure. He has worn his heart
on his sleeve so long, that it has hardened in the cold
air. He knows that his face is powdered, and if he
sobs, it is without tears ; and it is hard to distinguish,
under the chalk, if the grimace which twists his mouth
awry is mere laughter or mockery. He knows that

he is condemned to be always in public, that emotion would be supremely out of keeping with his costume, that he must remember to be fantastic if he would not be merely ridiculous. And so he becomes exquisitely false, dreading above all things that " one touch of nature " which would ruffle his disguise, and leave him defenceless. Simplicity, in him, being the most laughable thing in the world, he becomes learned, perverse, intellectualizing his pleasures, brutalizing his intellect ; his mournful contemplation of things becoming a kind of grotesque joy, which he expresses in the only symbols at his command, tracing his Giotto's O with the elegance of his pirouette.

" In more ways than one do men sacrifice to the rebellious angels," says St. Augustine ; and Beardsley's sacrifice, together with that of all great decadent art, the art of Rops or the art of Baudelaire, is really a sacrifice to the eternal beauty, and only seemingly to the powers of evil. And here let me say that I have no concern with what neither he nor I could have had absolute knowledge of, his own intention in his work. A man's intention, it must be remembered, from the very fact that it is conscious, is much less intimately himself than the sentiment which his work conveys to me. So large is the subconscious element in all artistic creation, that I should have doubted whether Beardsley himself knew what he intended to do, in this or that really significant drawing. Admitting that he could tell exactly what he had intended, I should be quite prepared to show that he had really done the very contrary. Thus when I say he was a profoundly spiritual artfst, though seeming to care chiefly for the manual part of his work ; that he expresses evil with an intensity which lifted it into a region almost of asceticism, though attempting, not seldom, little more than a joke or a caprice in line ; and that he was above all, though almost against his own will, a satirist, a satirist who has seen the ideal,— I am putting forward no paradox, nothing really contradictory, but a simple analysis of the work as it exists.

At times he attains pure beauty, has the unimpaired vision ; in the best of the *Salome* designs, here and there afterwards. From the first it is a diabolic beauty, but it is not yet divided against itself. The consciousness of sin is always there, but it is sin first transfigured by beauty, and then disclosed by beauty ; sin, conscious of itself, of its inability to escape itself, and showing in its ugliness the law it has broken. His world is a world of phantoms, in whom the desire of the perfecting of mortal sensations, a desire of infinity, has overpassed mortal limits, and poised them, so faint, so quivering, so passionate for flight, in a hopeless and strenuous immobility. They have the sensitiveness of the spirit, and that bodily sensitiveness which wastes their veins and imprisons them in the attitude of their luxurious meditation. They are too thoughtful to be ever really simple, or really absorbed by either flesh or spirit. They have nothing of what is " healthy " or merely " animal " in their downward course towards repentance ; no overwhelming passion hurries them beyond themselves ; they do not capitulate to an open assault of the enemy of souls. It is the soul in them that sins, sorrowfully, without reluctance, inevitably. Their bodies are faint and eager with wantonness ; they desire more pleasure than there is in the world, fiercer and more exquisite pains, a more intolerable suspense. They have put off the common burdens of humanity, and put on that loneliness which is the rest of saints and the unrest of those who have sinned with the intellect. They are a little lower than the angels, and they walk between these and the fallen angels, without part or lot in the world.

Here, then, we have a sort of abstract spiritual corruption, revealed in beautiful form ; sin transfigured by beauty. And here, even if we go no further, is an art intensely spiritual, an art in which evil purifies itself by its own intensity, and by the beauty which transfigures it. The one thing in the world which is without hope is that mediocrity which is the sluggish content of inert matter. Better be vividly awake to evil than, in mere somnolence, close the very issues and approaches of good and evil. For evil itself, carried to the point of a perverse ecstasy, becomes a kind of good, by means of that energy which, otherwise directed, is virtue ; and which can never, no matter how its course may be changed, fail to retain something of its original efficacy. The devil is nearer to God, by the whole height from which he fell, than the average man who has not recognized his own need to rejoice or to repent. And so a profound spiritual corruption, instead of being a more " immoral " thing than the gross and pestiferous humanity of Hogarth or of Rowlandson, is more nearly, in the final and abstract sense, moral, for it is the triumph of the spirit over the flesh, to no matter what end. It is a form of divine possession, by which the inactive and materializing soul is set in fiery motion, lured from the ground, into at least a certain high liberty. And so we find evil justified of itself, and an art consecrated to the revelation of evil equally justified ; its final justification being that declared by Plotinus, in his treatise *On the Nature of Good and Evil* :

" But evil is permitted to remain by itself alone on account of the superior power and nature of good ; because it appears from necessity everywhere comprehended and bound, in beautiful bands, like men fettered with golden chains, lest it should be produced openly to the view of divinity, or lest mankind should always behold its horrid shape when perfectly naked ; and such is the supervening power of good, that whenever a glimpse of perfect evil is obtained we are immediately recalled to the memory of good by the image of the beautiful with which evil is invested."

In those drawings of Beardsley which are grotesque rather than beautiful, in which lines begin to grow deformed, the pattern, in which now all the beauty takes refuge, is itself a moral judgment. Look at that drawing called *The Scarlet Pastorale*. In front, a bloated harlequin struts close to the footlights, outside the play, on which he turns his back ; beyond, sacramental candles have been lighted, and are guttering down in solitude, under an unseen wind. And between, on the sheer darkness of the stage, a bald and plumed Pierrot, holding in his vast, collapsing paunch with a mere rope of roses, shows the cloven foot, while Pierrette points at him in screaming horror, and the fat dancer turns on her toes indifferently. Need we go further to show how much more than Gautier's meaning lies in the old paradox of *Mademoiselle de Maupin,* that " perfection of line is virtue " ? That line which rounds the deformity of the cloven-footed sin, the line itself, is at once the revelation and

the condemnation of vice, for it is part of that artistic
logic which is morality.

Beardsley is the satirist of an age without convictions, and he can but paint hell as Baudelaire did,
without pointing for contrast to any contemporary
paradise. He employs the same rhetoric as Baudelaire,
a method of emphasis which it is uncritical to think
insincere. In that terrible annunciation of evil which
he called *The Mysterious Rose-Garden*, the lantern-
bearing angel with winged sandals whispers, from
among the falling roses, tidings of more than " pleasant sins." The leering dwarfs, the " monkeys," by
which the mystics symbolized the earthlier vices ;
those immense bodies swollen with the lees of pleasure,
and those cloaked and masked desires shuddering in
gardens and smiling ambiguously at interminable
toilets ; are part of a symbolism which loses nothing
by lack of emphasis. And the peculiar efficacy of
this satire is that it is so much the satire of desire
returning upon itself, the mockery of desire enjoyed,
the mockery of desire denied. It is because he loves
beauty that beauty's degradation obsesses him ; it is
because he is supremely conscious of virtue that vice
has power to lay hold upon him. And, unlike those
other, acceptable satirists of our day, with whom
satire exhausts itself in the rebuke of a drunkard
leaning against a lamp-post, or a lady paying the
wrong compliment in a drawing-room, he is the satirist
of essential things ; it is always the soul, and not the
body's discontent only, which cries out of these
insatiable eyes, that have looked on all their lusts, and
out of these bitter mouths, that have eaten the dust
of all their sweetnesses, and out of these hands, that

have laboured delicately for nothing, and out of these feet, that have run after vanities. They are so sorrowful because they have seen beauty, and because they have departed from the line of beauty.

And, after all, the secret of Beardsley is there; in the line itself rather than in anything, intellectually realized, which the line is intended to express. With Beardsley everything was a question of form: his interest in his work began when the paper was before him and the pen in his hand. And so, in one sense, he may be said never to have known what he wanted to do, while, in another, he knew very precisely indeed. He was ready to do, within certain limits, almost anything you suggested to him; as, when left to himself, he was content to follow the caprice of the moment. What he was sure of, was his power of doing exactly what he proposed to himself to do; the thing itself might be *Salome* or *Belinda*, *Ali Baba* or *Réjane*, the *Morte d'Arthur* or the *Rhinegold* or the *Liaisons Dangereuses*; the design might be for an edition of a classic or for the cover of a catalogue of second-hand books. And the design might seem to have no relation with the title of its subject, and, indeed, might have none: its relation was of line to line within the limits of its own border, and to nothing else in the world. Thus he could change his whole manner of working five or six times over in the course of as many years, seem to employ himself much of the time on trivial subjects, and yet retain, almost unimpaired, an originality which consisted in the extreme beauty and the absolute certainty of design.

It was a common error, at one time, to say that Beardsley could not draw. He certainly did not

draw the human body with any attempt at rendering
its own lines, taken by themselves ; indeed, one of
his latest drawings, an initial letter to *Volpone*, is
almost the first in which he has drawn a nude figure
realistically. But he could draw, with extraordinary
skill, in what is after all the essential way : he could
make a line do what he wanted it to do, express the
conception of form which it was his intention to express ; and this is what the conventional draughtsman,
Bouguereau, for instance, cannot do. The conventional
draughtsman, any Academy student, will draw a line
which shows quite accurately the curve of a human
body, but all his science of drawing will not make you
feel that line, will not make that line pathetic, as in the
little, drooping body which a satyr and a Pierrot are
laying in a puff-powder coffin, in the tailpiece to *Salome*.

And then, it must never be forgotten, Beardsley
was a decorative artist, and not anything else. From
almost the very first he accepted convention ; he set
himself to see things as pattern. Taking freely all that
the Japanese could give him, that release from the
bondage of what we call real things, which comes to
one man from an intense spirituality, to another from
a consciousness of material form so intense that it
becomes abstract, he made the world over again in
his head, as if it existed only when it was thus re-made,
and not even then, until it had been set down in black
line on a white surface, in white line on a black surface.
Working, as the decorative artist must work, in symbols
almost as arbitrary, almost as fixed, as the squares of a
chess-board, he swept together into his pattern all the
incongruous things in the world, weaving them into
congruity by his pattern. Using the puff-box, the
188

toilet-table, the ostrich-feather hat, with a full consciousness of their suggestive quality in a drawing of
archaic times, a drawing purposely fantastic, he put
these things to beautiful uses, because he liked their
forms, and because his space of white or black seemed
to require some such arrangement of lines. They were
the minims and crotchets by which he wrote down his
music; they made the music, but they were not the music.

In the *Salome* drawings, in most of *The Yellow Book*
drawings, we see Beardsley under this mainly Japanese
influence ; with, now and later, in his less serious
work, the but half-admitted influence of what was
most actual, perhaps most temporary, in the French
art of the day. *Pierrot gamin*, in *Salome* itself, altern-
ates, in such irreverences as the design of *The Black
Cape*, with the creator of noble line, in the austere and
terrible design of *The Dancer's Reward*, the ornate
and vehement design of *The Peacock Skirt*. Here
we get pure outline, as in the frontispiece ; a
mysterious intricacy, as in the border of the title-page
and of the table of contents ; a paradoxical beauty of
mere wilfulness, but a wilfulness which has its
meaning, its excuse, its pictorial justification, as in
The Toilette. *The Yellow Book* embroiders upon the
same manner ; but in the interval between the last
drawings for *The Yellow Book* and the first drawings
for *The Savoy*, a new influence has come into the work,
the influence of the French eighteenth century. This
influence, artificial as it is, draws him nearer, though
somewhat unquietly nearer, to nature. Drawings like
The Fruit Bearers, in the first number of *The Savoy*,
with its solid and elaborate richness of ornament, or
The Coiffing, in the third number, with its delicate

and elaborate grace, its witty concentration of line ; drawings like the illustrations to the *Rape of the Lock*, have, with less extravagance, and also a less strenuous intellectual effort, a new mastery of elegant form, not too far removed from nature while still subordinated to the effect of decoration, to the instinct of line. The four initial letters to *Volpone*, the last of which was finished not more than three weeks before his death, have a new quality both of hand and of mind. They are done in pencil, and they lose, as such drawings are bound to lose, very greatly in the reduced reproduction. But, in the original, they are certainly, in sheer technical skill, equal to anything he had ever done, and they bring at the last, and with complete success, nature itself into the pattern. And here, under some solemn influence, the broken line of beauty has reunited ; " the care is over," and the trouble has gone out of this no less fantastic world, in which Pan still smiles from his terminal column among the trees, but without the old malice. Human and animal form reassert themselves, with a new dignity, under this new respect for their capabilities. Beardsley has accepted the convention of nature itself, turning it to his own uses, extracting from it his own symbols, but no longer rejecting it for a convention entirely of his own making. And thus in his last work, done under the very shadow of death, we find new possibilities for an art, conceived as pure line, conducted through mere pattern, which, after many hesitations, has resolved finally upon the great compromise, that compromise which the greatest artists have made, between the mind's outline and the outline of visible things.

WHISTLER AND MANET

I

WHISTLER is dead, and there goes with him one of the greatest painters and one of the most original personalities of our time. He was in his seventieth year, and until quite lately seemed the youngest man in London. Unlike most artists, he was to be seen everywhere, and he was heard wherever he was seen. He was incapable of rest, and incapable of existing without production. When he was not working at his own art he was elaborating a fine art of conversation. In both he was profoundly serious, and in both he aimed at seeming to be the irresponsible butterfly of his famous signature. He deceived the public for many years ; he probably deceived many of his acquaintances till the day of his death. Yet his whole life was a devotion to art, and everything that he said or wrote proclaimed that devotion, however fantastically. I wish I could remember half the things he said to me, at any one of those few long talks which I had with him in his quiet, serious moments. I remember the dinner party at which I first met him, not many years ago, and my first impression of his fierce and impertinent chivalry on behalf of art. Some person officially connected with art was there, an urbane sentimentalist ; and after every official platitude there was a sharp crackle from Whistler's corner, and it was as if a rattlesnake had leapt suddenly out. The person did not know when he was dead, and Whistler transfixed him mortally, I know not how many times ; and still he smiled and talked. I had said something that pleased Whistler, and he peered at me with his old bright eyes from far down the room ; and after dinner he took me aside and talked to me for a full hour. He was not brilliant, or consciously clever, or one talking for effect ; he talked of art, certainly for art's sake, with the passionate reverence of the lover, and with the joyous certainty of one who knows himself beloved. In what he said, of his own work and of others, there was neither vanity nor humility ; he knew quite well what in his art he had mastered and what others had failed to master. But it was chiefly of art in the abstract that he talked, and of the artist's attitude towards nature and towards his materials. He only said to me, I suppose, what he had been saying and writing for fifty years ; it was his gospel, which he had preached mockingly, that he might disconcert the mockers ; but he said it all like one possessed of a conviction, and as if he were stating that conviction with his first ardour.

And the man, whom I had only before seen casually and at a distance, seemed to me almost preposterously the man of his work. At dinner he had been the controversialist, the acrobat of words ; I understood how this little, spasmodically alert, irritably sensitive creature of brains and nerves could never have gone calmly through life, as Rodin, for instance, goes calmly through life, a solid labourer at his task, turning neither to the right nor to the left, attending only to his own business. He was a great wit, and his wit was a personal expression. Stupidity hurt him, and he avenged himself for the pain. All his laughter was a crackling of thorns under the pot, but of flaming thorns, setting the pot in a fury of boiling. I never saw any one so feverishly alive as this little, old man, with his bright, withered cheeks, over which the skin was drawn tightly, his darting eyes, under their prickly bushes of eyebrow, his fantastically-creased black and white curls of hair, his bitter and subtle mouth, and, above all, his exquisite hands, never at rest. He had the most sensitive fingers I have ever seen, long, thin, bony, wrinkled, every finger alive to the tips, like the fingers of a mesmerist. He was proud of his hands, and they were never out of sight ; they travelled to his moustache, crawled over the table, grimaced in little gestures. If ever a painter had painter's hands it was Whistler. And his voice, with its strange accent, part American, part deliberately French, part tuned to the key of his wit, was not less personal or significant. There was scarcely a mannerism which he did not at one time or another adopt, always at least half in caricature of itself. He had a whole language of pauses, in the middle of a word or of a sentence, with all sorts of whimsical quotation-marks, setting a mocking emphasis on solemn follies. He had cultivated a manner of filling up gaps which did not exist ; " and so forth and so on," thrown in purely for effect, and to prepare for what was coming. A laugh, deliberately artificial, came when it was wanted ; it was meant to annoy, and annoyed, but needlessly.

He was a great wit, really spontaneous, so far as

what is intellectual can ever be spontaneous. His wit was not, as with Oscar Wilde, a brilliant sudden gymnastic, with words in which the phrase itself was always worth more than what it said ; it was a wit of ideas, in which the thing said was at least on the level of the way of saying it. And, with him, it was really a weapon, used as seriously as any rapier in an eternal duel with the eternal enemy. He fought for himself, but in fighting for himself he fought for every sincere artist. He spared no form of stupidity, neither the unintelligent stupidity of the general public, and of the critics who represent the public, nor the much more dangerous stupidity of intelligences misguided, as in the "leading case" of Ruskin. No man made more enemies, nor deserved better friends. He never cared, or was able, to distinguish between them. They changed places at an opinion or for an idea.

He was a great master of the grotesque in conversation, and the portrait which he made of Mr. Leyland as a many-tentacled devil at a piano, a thing of horror and beauty, is for once a verbal image put into paint, with that wholehearted delight in exuberant extravagance which made his talk wildly heroic. That painting is his one joke in paint, his one expression of a personal feeling so violent that it overcame his scruples as an artist. And yet even that is not really an exception ; for out of a malicious joke, begun, certainly, in anger, beauty exudes like the scent of a poisonous flower.

Many of his sayings are preserved, in which he seems to scoff at great artists and at great artistic qualities. They are to be interpreted, not swallowed.

His irreverence, as it was called, was only one, not easily recognizable, sign of a delicate sensitiveness in choice. And it had come to be one of the parts that he played in public, one of the things expected of him, to which he lent himself, after all, satirically. And he could be silent on occasion, very effectively. I happened to meet him one day in front of the Chigi *Botticelli*, when it was on view at Colnaghi's. He walked to and fro, peered into the picture, turned his head sideways, studied it with the approved air of one studying it, and then said nothing. " Why drag in Botticelli ? " was, I suppose, what he thought.

II

TASTE in Whistler was carried to the point of genius, and became creative. He touched nothing, possessed nothing, that he did not remake or assimilate in some faultless and always personal way : the frames of his pictures, the forms of the books which were printed for him, the shapes of the old silver which he collected, the arrangement of that silver when it was exhibited among other collections. The monogram which he designed for a friend who was a publisher is the simplest and the most decorative monogram that I can remember. He drew the lettering for the books of another friend, and this lettering, which seems the most obvious thing in the world, makes the lettering on every other modern book look clumsy or far fetched. And in none of these things does he try to follow a fine model or try to avoid following a model. He sees each thing in its own way, within its own limits.

No one ever had a more exact and reverent sense

of limits, a narrower and more variable standard of
perfection. He mastered, in his own art, medium
after medium, and his work, in each medium, is conspicuous for its natural sense of the canvas or the paper,
for its precise knowledge of exactly what can be done
with all the substances and materials of art. He never
sought novelty by confusing two methods, but made
the most of each with a tender and rigid economy.
When he paints, you distinguish the thread of his
canvas ; in his etchings and lithographs the meaning
of the design extends to the rim of the margin.

And of all modern painters he is the only one who
completely realized that a picture is part of the decoration of a wall, and of the wall of a modern room.
When pictures ceased to be painted on the walls of
churches and palaces, or for a given space above
altars, there came into the world that abnormal thing,
the easel-picture. At the present day there is only
one country in which the sense of decoration exists,
or is allowed to have its way ; and it was from the
artists of Japan that Whistler learnt the alphabet of
decorative painting. His pictures and his black-and-
white work are first of all pieces of decoration, and
there is not one which might not make, in the Japanese
way, the only decoration of a room.

Once, indeed, he was allowed, as no other great
artist of our time has been allowed, to decorate a room
for one of his own pictures. The Peacock Room
was made out of a gradual transformation, and it was
made as a sort of shrine for the lovely picture, *La
Princesse du Pays de la Porcelaine*. Every inch of the
wall, ceiling, and wainscoting, the doors, the frames
of the shutters, was worked into the scheme of the

blues and golds, and Mr. Leyland's china had its part, no doubt, in the scheme. But I do not think Whistler can be held responsible for the gilded cages (though, indeed, making the best of a bad bargain, he gilded them) which prop up the china round so much of the walls. These, I gather, he found already made, and with them he had to struggle : he accepted them frankly, and their glitter is a pretence on his part that he liked a room hung with bird-cages and plate-racks. But the gold peacocks on the shutters, with their solid and glowing fantasy of design, the gold peacocks on the blue leather of the wall facing the picture, with their dainty and sparkling fantasy of design, the sombre fantasy of the peacocks' feathers, untouched by gold, their colours repressed and with-drawn into shadow, above the lamps on the ceiling : all these, into which he put his very soul, which are so many signatures of his creed and science of beauty, are woven together into a web or network of almost alarming loveliness, to make a room into which nature, sunlight, or any mortal compromise could never enter, a wizard's chapel of art. Here, where he is least human, he joins with that other part of himself in which all his sense of what goes to make decoration mingled with another sense, completing it. When he is greatest, in the portrait of his mother, for instance, he is only more, and not less, decorative, as he gives you so infinitely much more than mere decoration. There is no compromise with taste in the abandon-ment to a great inspiration. Inspiration, with him, includes taste, on its way to its own form of perfection.

It was characteristic of Whistler that he should go to music for the titles of his pictures. A picture may

indeed be termed a *Nocturne*, even more justly than
a piece of music, but it was quite as it should be if
Chopin really was in Whistler's mind when he used
the word. Gautier had written his *Symphonie en
Blanc Majeur* before Whistler painted his *Symphonies
in White, Harmony in Grey and Green, Arrangement
in Black and Brown, Caprice in Purple and Gold* : all
are terms perfectly appropriate to painting, yet all
suggest music. And to the painter of Sarasate, music
could hardly have failed to represent the type of all
that his own art was aiming at, in its not always fully
understood or recognized way. In music, too, he had
his significant choice. I remember once his impatience
with my praise of Ysaye, whom he had never heard,
because the praise seemed like a poor compliment to
Sarasate, whose marvellous purity of tone he recalled
with an intolerant and jealous delight. He thought,
and was perhaps right in thinking, that there never
could have been a purer tone than Sarasate's, and the
rest mattered, at all events, much less.

And so, in speaking of Whistler's pictures, though
nothing so merely and so wholly pictorial was ever
done, it is musical terms that come first to one's mind.
Every picture has a purity of tone like that of the finest
violin playing. Sometimes a Giorgione, sometimes a
Watteau, comes to one as if in exchange for music ;
Whistler always.

III

THERE is an exhibition and you are asked merely to
see " some oil paintings by deceased masters." I like
the vague prose of the invitation, and I like to see

Whistler and Blake together, Goya and Richard Wilson, the school of Antwerp and the school of Siena. It is a relief to pass from one to another among no more than thirty-four pictures of such widely differing styles and periods. A few broad contrasts or comparisons may indeed strike one, but one is not teased into trying to weigh the merit of this with that picture, painted at the same time and with a similar intention. Bonifazio pleases me the more after I have looked at at early Turner, and from the *Dutch Babies* I pass with fresh curiosity to the strange faces of *Lord Rochester's Children*, the shy girl and sanctimonious boy. And there is a Blake which calls to one, among so many pictures painted with so much more of the craftsman's skill. Christ heals the blind man, a Christ reverently heightened, like a human pillar ; and the blind man is full of wonder and ardour as he staggers vehemently and uncertainly forward, and behind him is one of Blake's old men, like Samuel covered with a mantle, and coming up out of the grave ; and all the background is of hills, stained with mysterious light and sombre colours. But the picture which one sees first and returns to last, in this choice and varied collection, is the picture which hangs at the end of the room, Whistler's portrait of Connie Gilchrist, dancing with a skipping-rope. That picture was one of the portraits most conspicuously missing from the Whistler Exhibition. Even after the portrait of his mother, of Carlyle, of Miss Alexander, it needs to be seen, if one is to realize every corner of Whistler's genius as a portrait painter. It is different from any and, like the others, it is the creation of a pose. He reveals to us a little, exquisite, pathetic creature, caught in a moment of harmonious movement, as the feet touch the floor between two turns of the skipping-rope. It has passed, it is coming again, it turns in the air, and the thin childish body is arrested as if literally in the air ; a ghost of form in a ghost of movement.

In Whistler's portraits the pose itself is as much a part of the interpretation as the painting ; and the quality of a portrait such as the Sarasate is not to be judged, as it commonly is, by the apparent lack of seriousness in it. Boldini's startling portrait of Whistler himself was an example of the art which tries for this common kind of success ; there was the like-ness, and the shining hat, and as much real artistic sense as is contained in a flashlight. Even in Whistler's portrait of Comte de Montesquiou, a harlequin of letters, there was no actual harlequinade on the part of the painter, though he may have seemed indulgent to it in his model. How much less is there in the Sarasate, where a genuine artist, but not a pro-found artist, is seen making his astonishing appearance, violin in hand, out of darkness upon a stage where he is to be the virtuoso. Sarasate's tone is a miracle, like Melba's, and he added to this miracle of tech-nique a Southern fire, which used to go electrically through his audience. He has his temperament and his technique, nothing else. The man who holds the violin in his hands is a child, pleased to please ; not a student or a diviner. And Whistler has rendered all this, as truthfully as Watts rendered the very different problem of Joachim, in perhaps the greatest of his portraits. Joachim is in the act of playing ; he bends his brows over the music which he is studying, not reading ; if there is any platform

or any audience, he is unconscious of them ; he is
conscious only of Beethoven. Note how Sarasate
handles the violin. It is a child, a jewel. He is
already thinking of the sound, the flawless tone, not
of Beethoven, though he may be just going to play
the Kreutzer Sonata. Whistler has caught him, poised
him, posed him, another butterfly and alive. Imagine
Sarasate painted by Watts, or indeed in any way but
Whistler's. There might have been other great
pictures, but no other such interpretation.

And so, in this little dancer, who skips out of time
into eternity, more ghostly than flesh and blood, more
real than a dream ; this image and symbol of wavering,
unripe things, " sweet, not lasting," a toy, a perfume ;
we have another interpretation, not less subtle than
that of the childlike and wordy musician, an interpretation of the dancing-girl, which renders for our own
age something of what the Greek rendered on vases
and in marble reliefs for theirs. For our sophisticated
age that he may give its essence, he gives us the last
sophistication ; a girl travestied as a boy, and scarcely
a girl but a child, and a dance which mimics the games
of childhood. The clothes of the dancer are almost
of the same colour as the background, dull gold ;
only the incredibly thin legs dance out of the shadow,
in tights of pale gold ; and there is a spot of red in
each hand, in the handles of the skipping-rope. The
face, with its eyes like violets, looks out with calm-
ness that is a little old and a little weary ; it is the
child playing for other people's pleasure. As I think
of the picture the attitude comes back to me almost
like that of one condemned to gaiety and perpetual
motion, with something of cruelty in the insistence of

its light step. I have no doubt that the impression comes from the ambiguous air which Whistler gives to so many of his people ; a mystery which was part of his art, of his way of painting, as much as of his vision or intention.

Now look from this ghostly dancer to the solid woman who sits, so piercingly alive, in her white dress and with her knot of black curls, Goya's *Duchess of Alva*. Here is a living person, not evoked out of nothing, and left to waver between two lights, but a strong, actual and passionate woman of flesh and blood, thought out by the painter before he began to see her on his canvas, mastered, and then built up in a close copy of nature. It is queer, forbidding, not instantly interesting even ; reality not twisted into anything grim and fantastic, as in the wonderful miniatures on ivory which are to be seen in the same gallery. It is Goya creating in rivalry with nature, resolute not to go beyond nature's pattern. And, if you care to see how far skill of imitation can go, not a creation but a copy, look at the two *Dutch Babies* of Cornelius de Vos beside it ; a piece of homely comedy, an exact record of that comedy of nature which seems almost to force humour upon its copyist. What attentiveness, in the painter, to every fold and pucker in the flesh, and to the unconscious solemnity of the staring eyes ! We see the Dutchman's tenacious, friendly, and dispassionate observation ; and how strangely it contrasts with the Spaniard's eager heat and the nervous sensitiveness of the American.

To compare Manet and Whistler is to see two worlds of sight, and it is possible to pass from the one to the other without more than a personal preference ;

they are on an equality. Each reveals himself in his
etchings, not less distinctly than in his pictures, though
Whistler's etchings extend over thirty years, while
Manet's were done for the most part between 1860
and 1866. In the work of Manet his etchings are
almost an accident, while in Whistler's they are an
essential part of the work. But in these thirty etchings,
only six of which are on the walls, and the others are
to be seen in a portfolio, one sees the real, the characteristic Manet, his simplicity of sight, over against
Whistler's subtlety ; his hard outline, his sense of
form, over against the colour and wavering outline
of Whistler. Look at the *Olympia* almost as fine as
the picture itself ; with its strong grip on darkness ;
the three cats, placed with astonishing decision, each
in its place ; the *Berthe Morisot*, a masterpiece of
character-drawing, and the *Eva Gonzalès*, a miracle
of suggested form and character, in mere big scrawl
of outline. Perhaps the most delightful as a picture
is *La Queue à la Boucherie*, done in 1871, and certainly
nothing is more brilliant in its dexterity than the last
of all, the *Jeanne* of 1882. Occasionally, as in *L'Acteur
tragique*, we feel a kind of rhetoric in the emphasis ;
as we feel, very disagreeably, and for a reason, in the
head of Poe. Compare this conventional portrait,
done after a photograph, with the startling Baudelaire
and the splendid Banville done from life ; and you
will see what happens when Manet has not the model
under his eye. There is a *Marine*, a fantastic ship
on a fantastic sea, which is just such another attempt
to put something invented and imaginary in the place
of a real thing ardently seen. For the most part these
are studies of Spanish actors, people who are studies

of Spanish dancers and Spanish actors, people who helped Manet to realize Spain before he went there, but when he was already under the influence of Spanish painting. They have the sombre elegance, poise and pungency of Spanish people ; and Manet and Baudelaire have had each an equal share in immortalizing that dancer, Lola de Valence, whom Manet's etching shows us, all nervous energy and arrested movement, while, in Baudelaire's stanza :

> On voit scintiller en Lola de Valence,
> Le charme inattendu d'un bijou rose et noir.

And there are pictures of old men smoking, of a boy blowing bubbles, of a kneeling youth drinking out of a gourd (one of the best), and a *Toilette* which may have led the way to Degas. In all these the beauty is a form of energy, and comes out of the fresh unflinching way in which a very ordinary thing is seen and captured. It is singular to remember that there was a time not so many years ago, when Manet was looked upon as wildly eccentric ; he seems to us now so simple, so straightforward, so obvious almost in his aim at truth. What Whistler aims at is an aspect much more cunningly chosen, a rarity of aspect, in which the thing may be caught off-guard, and set, dainty and unexpected, before one. In his real and rare world, indicated well enough by these fifteen etchings of many periods, there is only one failure to achieve exactly what he had meant to do, the exact shade of beauty ; the St. James's Street, which means for Whistler very little. But in these examples of Venice, Dutch and French sets, in the Thames etchings, and in the portraits, we see the Whistler who

MANET

L'Odalisque

was one of the lyric poets of sight. Only Rembrandt, among etchers, was a greater poet; and even Rembrandt was only greater in the sense in which Milton is greater than Crashaw.

IV

IT has been said by a penetrating and suggestive French critic, Charles Morice, that the course of Fantin-Latour, in his work, was traced " from the real world to the dream-world through a garden." He began, it is true, in the 'sixties, with studies from life and lithographs from mythology, both together; but, in the main, the " realistic work " (the portraits and the flower-pieces) was done earlier than the studies from music and from dreams. In certain pictures we see work of each period, very fairly representative; and we see by a glance at the exquisite *Portrait of the Artist's Sister*, painted in 1861, that whatever quality of really pictorial imagination can be distinguished in the late, more professedly " ideal " work, is already implicit, and we may think in a more satisfying measure, in the earliest, when the artist has not yet grown tired of the visible world.

Everyone who has ever entered the Luxembourg will remember the picture which represents Manet painting in his studio, with Zola and a group of friends standing around him. How good it is, how trustworthy, how searching in its study of all these types of the artist; but, at the same time, how chilling to the eyes. It is not a thing caught just thus, but a collection of people painted one by one, and set there very intelligibly before us. Fantin never saw the visible world as it was, even in these early portraits after nature, or in the early studies of still-life. He loves flowers, but individual flowers plucked and put in glasses, not a landscape, which scarcely occurs in his work ; definite objects, like the white cup and saucer (No. 8), which he makes into a beautiful thing, all by itself ; carefully chosen faces, mostly those of one kind or another of artist, each very carefully individualized, as in that *Coin de Table*, which has preserved for us the face of the young Rimbaud. It is not a way of seeing reality, but a way of picking certain choice things, a flower, a fruit, a face, out of reality, and reproducing just that, just as it is. Finally, and as a natural consequence of this selection (to which he adds copies of great pictures, which are like interpretations), he can find nothing any longer in reality that contents him, and he takes refuge in dreams, among wild lights and supernatural gleams, among phantoms of poets and musicians, Wagner, Berlioz, Byron, Schumann ; himself most like Schumann, a cloudy dreamer, to whom Astarte comes on a cadence that is like moonlight. He has always sought rarity, and now he seeks ecstasy, which he would fain transpose from other arts into his own art ; he would find short cuts to ecstasy, being a little tired of all there is to pore over and copy in the single flower, the single face. The lithographs snatch a filled cup too hastily and part of the music is spilled.

Among Fantin's paintings there are a few in which an imaginative conception, finely mysterious, is rendered with a certain dull glow of colour, really, in the true sense, lyrical. In *La Danse*, where the veiled shapes are brought out into sudden light, it is as if morning had come upon a dream. There is no longer beauty to divine, but something very like prettiness to see ; and in such late pictures as the *Aurora* and the *Venus and Cupid*, something waxy and almost like a trail of Bouguereau comes between the painter and his vision. In the lithographs, which are mostly dedicated to music, an attempt to render the essence of, for instance, the Prelude to *Lohengrin* in a design, there is invention, always in a sense pictorial, but rarely, I think, on a level, as pictorial invention, with the music which it sets itself to interpret. Looking at that particular design, I see a very ingenious translation from sound into visible outline ; it is intelligible at once, one approves it critically, as a conception, but one cannot abandon oneself to what it says with these shapes, upward motions and scattered lights, as one can to the vast and exquisite ebb and flow of the tidal music. The lithographs are all romantic, in a Byronic or 1830 sense, a little operatic even ; and they cannot take themselves lightly, as decoration, or mere whim ; they are almost German in their emotional seriousness, or, as in *Le Poète et la Muse*, out-rhetoric French rhetoric.

To go from the company of the Fantin-Latours to the company of the Whistlers is to pass suddenly from a world never quite real into a world as real as day and night. It is a world in which I, for one, find almost everything that I have ever cared to see, or to linger over, in what we call the real world. Here, at least, I see through a painter's vision the world which I have always lived in, a world which is full of beautiful appearances, and which, with all its fullness and satisfaction, is only a shadow and symbol of some supreme beauty, which we can see only through that shadow, but which is assuredly enough for one life. It is Whistler's reality that astonishes me the most, and the variety with which he represents that reality, going clean through outward things to their essence, that is, to their essential reality ; never, like Fantin, setting up an invention in the place of nature. It is remarkable that an artist who may seem, in his words, to have denied nature, or to have put himself arrogantly in the place of nature, should, in his pictures, have given us no image, no outline, no shade or colour, which is not evoked out of a thing really seen and delicately remembered. Tracing the course of these pictures from first to last one sees the technique changing from what is in a sense a realistic to what seems an evasive manner ; from the Courbet-like *Wave* of 1861 with its shouldering strength and heavy paint to the *Nocturne, Blue and Green* of the Thames water asleep, or to those aspects of people and things in which a butterfly seems to have left a little of its coloured dust on a flower as it alights and passes.

Each comes closer than the last to something really seen, but with a vision more and more subtle and stealthy. He begins by building his world after nature's, with supports as solid and as visible. Gradually he knocks away support after support, expecting the structure to support itself by its own consciousness, so to speak, at the perfect moment he gives to the eye just enough to catch in the outlines of things that it may be able to complete them by that imaginative sympathy which is part of the seeing of works of art. But he can never be content with that service, and demands ever more and more of it in his challenge with

MANET
The Picnic

things, with himself. And he comes finally to suppose that, after all, eyes have the sight and sensitiveness of his own ; which is as if one were to expect the A B C class to read Euclid off the blackboard. The attitude towards Whistler of the older critics and of the public of yesterday was that of a rather vulgar curiosity. He had shown them a glimpse, and they wanted a gulp ; and they pressed close to the canvas to see what a policeman sees when he turns his bull's-eye on the lock of a door. But the closer they got the less they saw, and they went away in a rage and said there was nothing to see. A great man did a great wrong by doing that : the picture which he thought a pot of paint flung on the face of the public is, to-day, exquisite in its beauty ; and what Ruskin could do seemed to receive a sanction for the public which had just got far enough to see Ruskin. The other picture, which Burne-Jones bore witness against, is to be seen, the *Nocturne in Blue and Silver*, and I had been sitting in front of it for a long time, drinking in its cool and remote harmony with unusual delight, before someone came up to me and told me that it was this picture which seemed to Burne-Jones (who yet had a sense of humour) like a bad joke. Vulgar curiosity is never gratified in any of Whistler's pictures. He never stared at nature, and you must not stare at his pictures. He treated nature as a gentleman treats a lady, and his fine manners were rewarded by exquisite revelations. I am sure that when he was painting a portrait he tried not to see his sitter, but to let that sitter surprise him, as a delicate artist in words lets himself be surprised by ideas, each surprise being like a sudden light. There is always a certain stealth about magic, and the magical quality did not come into Whistler's pictures by a forthright effort. But he prepared for it, and with ceremony, as one prepares for the reception of a guest.

Among Whistler's works there are nearly a hundred paintings in oil, with a smaller number of drawings in water-colours and pastel and black and white, more than two hundred lithographs, and almost five hundred and fifty etchings. Into such a world, so variously beautiful, one cannot enter rashly or walk there hastily. To attempt to realize it at once in detail would be like trying to crowd sixty moments of separate ecstasy into a single hour.

V

IT is a rare accident which has allowed us to see the most complete exhibition which has yet been made of Whistler's pictures within a week of the closing of the most complete exhibition which has yet been made of the pictures of Watts. Each has his own world. Watts paints always with a sense of the glory of the work, of human glory, of the supreme glory of the spirit, or of God, which maketh all these lesser glories. No detail stops his vision, or puts out his hand, which sweeps freely, at home among splendours. His is a kind of heroic work, in which there is only nobility and affluence ; every colour and every contour is noble and ample, only sometimes the painter's enthusiasm for things loses the subtler beauties which are in them, and so loses truth, as well as this more intimate beauty, by this way. He paints, certainly, the world he lives in ; and what more can anyone ask of any painter ?

Whistler, too, has his own world, which is neither splendid nor affluent, but an exquisite and exact world of shapes and shades, evoked with certainty and aloofness, the artist's aloofness from the aspects which he chooses for his own pleasure, out of visible things. And, in his disinterested greediness, which would follow and capture the whole of his own part of the work, he experiments with many mediums, and has many manners, though only one style. Each of his pictures has its " minutely appropriate " beauty, its " minutely appropriate " handling. In *The Blue Wave* we see him literally working with Courbet, and this, like the Breton seascape, and the building of Westminster Bridge, has the direct, almost violent truthfulness of Courbet. In *At the Piano* we have all that was most significant in the Pre-Raphaelite movement summed up ; the *Shipping in the Thames* with the pale greys and pinks, the ghost of a landscape, is pure Puvis de Chavannes ; in *The Purple Cap* we get all Albert Moore, and how much besides ! Whatever *The White Girl* owed to Rossetti was a debt already paid before the picture was finished. Japan and Velasquez, whenever they are seen, are seen through creative eyes. And just as in the landscapes and seascapes we see the paint thinning, clarifying, becoming more and more exquisitely and exactly expressive, so in the portraits and figure pieces we can trace the elimination of effort, the spiritualizing of paint itself ; in the white, for instance—cold in *The White Girl* of 1862, more luminous in the third. *Symphony in White* of 1867, and finally, in the *Miss Alexander* of the early 'seventies, a white which is like the soul of a colour, caught and fixed there by some incalculable but precisely calculated magic. It ends, of course, by being the ghost of a colour, as in *The Convalescents*, but all things in Whistler end, when their particular life is over, by becoming the ghosts of themselves. All Whistler's portraits are at once disquietingly real, and at the same time perfect pieces of decoration, in which the pattern loses nothing because it is made out of a living thing. And no two of the portraits are alike, but each is surrounded by precisely his or her individual atmosphere ; each lives with a reality which is unlike the reality of any other. It is enough to look from the portrait of Carlyle to the portrait of Sarasate, and from that to the portrait of Duret. Does not Carlyle live grimly, and as if angrily silent in the empty room ? and Sarasate, poised airily as if he heard the music of the violin in his hands ·before he drew the bow across it, emerging out of darkness ? And Duret, a solid figure, correct, mundane, with the pink domino held like a bibelot. Each is an evocation, and each interprets, while seeming to exist only for the lines or colours of an artist's fancy. It was part of Whistler's wise method to declare his indifference, as a painter, to what might be thought the " meaning," in literary terms of anything that he painted, but has he not said also that in portrait-painting it is for the artist " to put on canvas something more than the face the model wears for that one day ; to paint the man, in short, as well as his features " ? It is the aim of Whistler, as of so much modern art, to be taken at a hint, divined at a gesture, or telepathy. Mallarmé, suppressing syntax and punctuation, the essential link of things, sometimes fails in his incantation, and brings before us things homeless and unattached in middle air. Verlaine subtilizes

words in a song to a mere breathing of music. And so
in Whistler there are problems to be guessed, as well
as things to be seen. But that is because these exceptional, difficult movements of nature, these twilight
aspects, the re-glimpses in which one sees hardly
more than a colour, no shape at all, or shapes covered
by mist or night, or confused by sunlight, have come
to seem to him the only aspect worth caring about.
Without " strangeness in its proportion " he can no
longer see beauty, but it is the rarity of beauty, always,
that he seeks, never a strange thing for the sake of
strangeness ; so that there is no eccentricity, as there
is no display, in his just and reticent records. If he
paints artificial light, it is to add a new, strange beauty
to natural objects, as night and changing lights really
add to them ; and he finds astonishing beauties in the
fireworks at Cremorne Gardens, in the rockets that fall
into the blue water under Battersea Bridge. They are
things beautiful in themselves, or made beautiful by
the companionship and co-operation of the night ; in
a picture they can certainly be as beautiful as stars and
sunsets. A picture is finished, said Whistler, " when
all trace of the means used to bring about the end has
disappeared." No one so rarely failed to know when
that moment had come ; but in two studies of a model
on a couch, of which one is called a completed, and the
other an incompleted print, it is the uncompleted
which is the finer, and every added touch of colour a
cheapening of the magic. It was part of the taste
raised to genius in Whistler that he almost invariably
knew when to stop. Look at a tiny, indistinct sketch
in water-colour on tinted paper. It is nothing and it
is enough, for it is a moment of faint colour, as satisfy-

ing in itself as one of those moments of faint colour
which we see come and go in the sky after sunset.
All the little water-colours are among the things that
no one but Whistler has ever been able to do in painting ; Verlaine has done the equivalent thing in poetry.
They have their brief coloured life like butterflies, and
with the same momentary perfection. No one had
ever cared to preserve just these aspects, as no one
before Verlaine had ever cared to sing certain bird
notes. Each was satisfied when he had achieved the
particular, delicate beauty at which he had aimed ;
neither cared or needed to go on, add the foot-note to
the text, enclose the commentary within the frame,
as most poets and painters are considerate enough
to do.

In the etchings and in the lithographs we see two
worlds, each a peopled world of its own : the world
of the etchings more precise, as of a real world seen,
however choicely, in terms of literal reality ; the other,
a more vaporous world, in which things and people are
seen with softer outlines, in an atmosphere more wholly
that of twilight. It is rare in either to come across
anything that can be said to have a subject, like the
early etching of *The Miser*. The subject was in the
aspect, and Whistler finds it just as well and as ade-
quately for his purpose in the *Lobster Pots*, or in the
Savoy Scaffolding. The real secret of Whistler, I
think, is this ; that he does not try to catch the accident
when an aspect becomes effective, but the instant
when it becomes characteristically beautiful. Take his
miraculous lithograph of Mallarmé, that slight sketch,
as it seems, for which he had forty sittings, and which
looks as if it had been done in half an hour. Manet's

portrait used to hang by the side of Whistler's at
Mallarmé's ; but even Manet, who could do so many
things that Whistler could not do, had not caught the
poet of the *Faun* at that precise moment into which
Whistler had caught him and in which he had revealed
the course and significance of a lifetime. Manet is
without strangeness, he sees with tenacity under the
absolute guidance of light ; but with Whistler it is hit
or miss, a nervous trial of skill which, like the acrobats,
must succeed almost every time, as if his life also were
staked upon it.

V I

THE Triumph of Whistler has been one of the great
and conspicuous triumphs in our time of genius over
prejudice, of genuine and original genius over false
conventional art. The painters and the art critics,
and the official persons and the man in the street were
against Whistler from the first ; he flourished his
painting in their faces as the banderillero flourishes his
red cloak in the face of the bull. It is the death of the
bull, one of the recurrent and propitiatory deaths of the
eternal and sacrificed bull, and we celebrate in the
purchase for the nation on the part of the National Art
Collections Fund of a picture of Whistler which was
once derided in a British Law Court with Ruskin and
Burne-Jones, each an honest man of genius, bearing
false witness against it.

Whistler, of course, delayed his public triumph by
his impatience for it. He had not the strength to be
patient, sit still and wait. He thought he " did well
to be angry," because he saw himself in the light of a

215

martyr for principles or of the imprisoned Galileo. His little poisoned arrows, that rankled but did not kill, kept up a guerrilla warfare really on behalf of justice, though they might seem to be shot from under cover of wounded vanity. It is idle to say that they did not do havoc among the enemies, though they kept the fighter too long under the flag of a bandit.

Whistler by his writing did for art in England something like what Poe did for literature in America. Those criticisms of the *literati*, which we read to-day with such a sense of labour wasted, helped to scour New York of scum, but they kept Poe back from recognition as the one great impersonal artist whom America has produced. His anger was a scourge for fools, and the fools cast back mud. Some of the mud stuck, and seemed to discredit him in the eyes of the fine gentlemen of the moment. It seems even now, as if we must forgive something to the artist because he condescended to be a fighter. Just as Whistler made it a little difficult for persons of limited comprehension to abandon themselves to the charm and magic of his canvases because they saw in front of them a nimble duellist, whom they called Jimmy, keeping his paintbrush in the air " like a dancer."

Whistler kept back his own triumph, but the national forces of things may be trusted to keep back the recognition of any new truth or beauty which comes into the world. Blake said, in one of the wisest of his scraps of divine doggerel :

Some people admire the work of a fool,
For it's sure to keep your judgment cool ;
It does not reproach you with want of wit ;
It is not like a lawyer serving a writ !

Truth and beauty come upon the unprepared and the indifferent " like a lawyer serving a writ." They come to accuse and to awaken the world, not to gratify the world in its sleep. It is not tragic that the better must always be the enemy of the good, and that the fittest should survive by the destruction of what was once fittest. Youth and beauty are hungry harpies, toothed and clawed, parricides and matricides, or, if they do not kill their parents, they thrust them out of doors, helpless with age.

The painting of Whistler came at a time when the public was beginning to accustom itself to the minute religion of the eyes which the Pre-Raphaelites had brought in ; and the public, though it may have many loves contemporaneously, can have but one creed at a time. Ruskin by much preaching had brought the public to its knees ; it was not convinced that it liked Pre-Raphaelite pictures, but it was certain that its duty to its higher self condemned it to accept them as what it ought to like. Imagine a poor public convinced that the manner of " the awakened conscience " was the manner of all great art, and then brought face to face with this particular *Battersea Bridge*, which seemed to it a wavering blue ghost, a trick of moonshine, the imposition of a juggler ! There are still people who are so little able to use their eyes that they cannot see the absolute " truth to nature " of that picture ; and how many painters since that time, besides Whistler, have been training the natural timidity of the eyes, leading it to see more than it had ever believed, and to believe in the long run whatever it could see. Here was a choice of subject, a way of painting, which had no relation with those devout details of the older school ; and if the one was religion, the other, certainly, must be heresy. So said the public, and so, alas ! said Ruskin. And so Whistler has to wait for the new eyes of the new generation ; and he had to train the sight of those eyes, to accustom them to take in new images of familiar objects, so every great original painter has had to do in every generation.

AUGUSTE RODIN

I

I MET Auguste Rodin in Paris, 182 rue de l'Université, in May, 1892. The last time that I saw him was at a dinner given in Old Burlington Street in 1907. No one who has seen him can ever forget his singular appearance. There before me stood a giant of genius, with the timidity of the colossus ; with a face in which strength struggled with passion ; with veiled blue eyes that dilated like the eyes of a parrot when he spoke of anything that interested him deeply. He made few gestures ; only when he sat, with his great hands folded on his knees, the gestures he made were for a purpose, never for an effect. I was struck by his quietness, his simplicity, a certain caution which comes from a suspicion that he is not being taken simply enough. When he talked of books or of his art or of nature there was always the same freshness and profundity.

It was in Meudon, in 1903, that Rodin spoke to me about Gustave Moreau. He said Moreau was a man of science, one of a generation which was taught to study art in the galleries, and not from nature. He was a great combiner. He took colour from Delacroix, his figures from the antique. He was not a genius, not a creator, not the great artist some have called him, but he belongs to the second rank. His greatest defect was that the figures which should be the principal part of the composition were uninteresting ; the detail and the surroundings took up most of his interest. *Il était froid au fond*, said Rodin.

He spoke to me of Stéphane Mallarmé's conversation and his way of writing—full of foreshortening—" many people don't understand foreshortening." Certainly Mallarmé, whom I met later, used in his later work this artistic heresy. Imagine his poem written down, at least composed. With this most writers would be content, but with Mallarmé the work has only begun. He works over it, word by word, changing a word here, for its colour, which is not precisely the colour required, a word there, for the break it makes in the music. A new image occurs to him, rarer, subtler than the one he has used ; the image is transferred. By the time the poem has reached, as it seems to him, a flawless unity, the steps of the progress have been only too effectually effaced ; and while the poet, who has seen the unity from the beginning, still sees the relation of point to point, the reader, who comes to it only in its final stage, finds himself in a not unnatural bewilderment. Pursue this manner of writing to its ultimate development ; start with an enigma, and then withdraw the key of the enigma ; and you arrive, easily, at the frozen impenetrability of those latest sonnets in which the absence of all punctuation is scarcely a recognizable hindrance.

He spoke to me also of modern dress ; what could be done with it ? It all depends on the suggestion of the nude underneath the clothes. The beauty of woman's costume is that the woman is underneath, and lends it some of her life. It makes him sad to see

RODIN
Beauty—Sketch

old clothes hanging in shop-windows—they seem so empty of life, waiting to become alive. He spoke of the way in which the nude is suggested here, simplified by some fine sweep. He has not done it because he has been engaged in other work and so has had no time even to attempt it. It can never be as great as the nude, but the eighteenth century had shown that it can be delightful.

When I first saw him he said to me that his secret consisted in *exaggeration* : that in this way he gets his effects without any of the hardness of other sculptors. As he showed me his mysterious little statue—the man kneeling so strangely in adoration before the woman in whom is imaged the sphinx and the child—he said to me : " Tell me what it means—what is your impression ? "

" *Le mystère de l'amour,*" I said.

I saw the *Danaid* slightly enlarged, with its wonderful flesh, the palpitation of the very dimples. Certainly no one but Rodin has been so tender with women in his exquisite creations ; none has ever caught so much of the eternal feminine as this sculptor of Hell. I saw the bust of Puvis de Chavannes in marble, wonderfully modelled ; the lines of the neck coming out like real flesh, the modelling of the ear, the lines of the face. Yet in so wonderful a poise of the head one saw the ability of the expression of nullity : the look of a man who goes through a crowd and sees nothing.

When one has realized what is called the *colouring* of his statues, in a sense like that of painting, the cunning employment of shadows, the massing, the conception that begins them, the achievement that ends them, one sees little enough of the infinite secrets of this man of genius. Let me choose, for instance, the exquisitely enlaced couple where a youth and a maiden are clasped in a virginal embrace—the shadow of the hair falling along his cheeks—with so lovely and discreet a shadow, when the lips press the hair of the maiden ; her face is blotted out under his cheek : one sees it, lost in ecstasy, behind. And in these who lie in a space of small rock, one sees the exquisite purity of the flesh, the daring of the pose, foot pressed amorously on foot : the very down of the flesh.

So, in the two qualities I have named, sweetness and strength, he is allied with Michelangelo. " For to his true admirers," wrote Pater, " there are sweetness and strength, pleasure with surprise, an energy of conception which seems at any moment about to break through all the conditions of comely grace, recovering, touch by touch, a loveliness found usually only in the simplest natural things—*ex forti dulcedo*."

Yet, in this epic in stone, stone becomes song, becomes music. And in its perfect proportions, in its harmonies, in its balance (composed of so many exquisite poems massed together) how lyric art becomes a great drama ! And there is a definite reason for comparing this creation of Rodin's with both the lyrical and the dramatic arts. Did he not say to me, did he not write, of the architecture of the human body, " that it is architecture, and that architecture is comparable with it " ? " Moving architecture," as he calls it in his book, " and so simple, if one possesses the secret of it, that it hurts one's eyes and yet one must see it." But, he said to me with his deep laugh, " instead of giving me my due as a sculptor—as to the quality of my work—they say I am a poet. Of course, when one is inspired one is a poet. Yet when they say that my inspiration gives a certain value to the theory of the poet neighbouring on folly, there they are wrong. *Je suis le contraire d'un exalté.*"

In regard to this saying I asked him why he had represented Hugo naked, and he said : " *C'est plus beau.*" Then he said : " It is for the Panthéon—a man in modern dress would not be in keeping there." I give here the stanza I wrote on *Le Penseur* :

> Out of eternal bronze and mortal breath,
> And to the glory of man, me Rodin wrought
> Before the gates of glory and of death
> I bear the burden of the pride of thought.

I I

THE art of Rodin competes with nature rather than with the art of other sculptors. Other sculptors turn life into sculpture, he turns sculpture into life. His clay is part of the substance of the earth, and the earth still clings about it as it comes up and lives. It is at once the flower and the root ; that of others is the flower only, and the plucked flower. That link with the earth, which we find in the unhewn masses of rock from which his finest creations of pure form can never quite free themselves, is the secret of his deepest force. It links his creations to nature's, in a single fashion of growth.

Rodin is a visionary, to whom art has no meaning apart from truth. His first care is to assure you, as you penetrate into that bewildering world which lies about him in his studios, that every movement arrested in those figures, all in violent action, is taken straight from nature. It is not copied, as you or I would see it ; it is re-created, as he sees it. How then does he see nature ? To Rodin everything that lives is beautiful, merely because it lives, and everything is equally beautiful.

Rodin believes, not as a mystic, but as a mathematician, I might almost say, in that doctrine of " correspondences " which lies at the root of most of the mystical teaching. He spies upon every gesture, knowing that if he can seize one gesture at the turn of the wave, he has seized an essential rhythm of nature. When a woman combs her hair, he will say to you, she thinks she is only combing her hair : no, she is making a gesture which flows into the eternal rhythm, which is beautiful because it lives, because it is part of that geometrical plan which nature is always weaving for us. Change the gesture as it is, give it your own conception of abstract beauty, depart ever so little from the mere truth of the movement, and the rhythm is broken, what was living is dead.

We speak of the rhythm of nature. What is it, precisely, that we mean ? Rhythm, precisely, is a balance, a means of preserving equilibrium in moving bodies. The human body possesses so much volume, it has to maintain its equilibrium ; if you displace its contents here, they shift there : the balance is regained by an instinctive movement of self-preservation. Thus what we call harmony is really utility, and, as always, beauty is seen to be a necessary thing, the exquisite growth of a need. And this rhythm runs through all nature, producing every grace and justifying every apparent defect. [The same swing and balance of forces make the hump on a dwarf's back and the mountain in the lap of a plain. One is not more beautiful than the other, if you will take each thing simply, in its own place. And that apparent ugliness of the average, even, has its place, does not require the heightening energy of excess to make it beautiful. It, too, has the beauty of life.]

There was a time, Rodin will tell you, when he sought for beautiful models ; when he found himself disappointed, dissatisfied, before some body whose proportions did not please him. He would go on working merely because the model was there ; and, after two hours' work, discover suddenly the beauty of this living thing which was turning into a new kind of life under his fingers. Why choose any longer ? why reject this always faultless material ? He has come to trust nature so implicitly that he will never pose a model, leaving nature to find its own way of doing what he wants of it. All depends on the way of seeing, on the seizure of the perfect moment, on the art of rendering, in the sculptor's relief, " the instant made eternity."

Rodin was studying drawing, with no idea but of being a draughtsman, when the idea of modelling in clay came to him. He had been drawing the model from different points of view, as the pivot turned, presenting now this and now that profile. It occurred to him to apply this principle to the clay, in which, by a swift, almost simultaneous, series of studies after nature, a single figure might be built up which would seem to be wholly alive, to move throughout its entire surface. From that time until now, he has taken one profile after another, each separately, and all together, turning his work in all directions, looking upward at the model to get the arch and hollow of the eyebrows, for instance, looking down on the model, taking each angle, as if, for the time, no other existed, and pursuing the outlines of nature with a movement as constant as her own. At the end, the thing is done, there is no need of even a final point of view, of an adjustment to some image of proportion : nature has been caught on the wing, enfolded by observation as the air enfolds the living form. If every part is right, the whole must be right.

But, for the living representation of nature in movement, something more is needed than the exact copy. This is a certain deliberate exaggeration ; not a correction, not a deviation, but a means of interpretation, the only means by which the softness and the energy of nature can be rendered in clay. It is a manner of expressing in clay what nature expresses with the infinite resources of its moving blood. " All art," said Mérimée, " is exaggeration *à propos*." It is on the perfection of this *à propos* that everything depends, and here Rodin's training as a draughtsman gives him his safety in freedom. He, who never measures his proportions, can rely implicitly on the exactitude of his eye, in preserving the proportion of every exaggeration.

When *l'Age d'Airain*, the bronze which is now in the Luxembourg, was sent to the Salon of 1877, Rodin was accused by the hanging committee of having moulded it on a living model. He protested, there was an official inquiry, and the commissioners came to the conclusion that at least some parts of the body had been thus moulded. It was not until three years later that the charge was finally disproved and officially withdrawn ; the statue was again exhibited at the Salon, a

medal of the third class awarded to it, and it was afterwards bought by the State. The story is instructive,
and might be remembered by those who have since
brought against Rodin so very different an accusation.
Turn from this statue to the marvellous little bronze of
la Vieille Heaulmière : there, in that re-incarnation of
Villon's ballade, you will see the same precision of
anatomical design, with an even deeper sense of the
beauty of what age and the horror of decay cannot
take out of the living body. Rodin has never taken a
step without knowing exactly where he is going to set
his foot, and he has never turned back from a step once
taken. It was not until he could copy nature so exactly
as to deceive the eyes of those who imagined that they
knew nature when they saw it, it was not until he had
the body by heart, that he began to make the body
think. He had given it form ; the form must be
awakened. The touch of life and of thought comes,
then, from an exaggeration here, an exaggeration there ;
a touch, inexplicable and certain, which is at once his
method and his secret.

It is on these two methods that Rodin relies for the
rendering of his vision of life. The art of the sculptor
gives him but one means of expression ; all is in relief,
all depends on the power, balance, and beauty of the
relief. Watching the living movement from every
angle, turning about it as a wild beast turns about its
prey, spying for the moment to pounce, seize, and
possess, he must translate form, movement, light and
shadow, softness, force, everything which exists in
nature, by the cunning adjustment of his relief. " Le
style, c'est l'homme," we say ; " le modelé, c'est l'art,"
Rodin would say.

Rodin has sometimes been compared with Michelangelo, but it would be more accurate to trace the principles of his art back to the Greeks. The Greeks worked directly from nature, with a fresh observation, the eyesight of the youth of the world, and its unspoilt mastery of hand. In Donatello we find the same directness, less powerful but not less sincere. Michelangelo approached nature through Donatello, so to speak, and then departed from nature, with his immense confidence, his readiness to compete with nature itself on a scale more decoratively impressive than nature's. His exaggeration is not the exaggeration of the Greeks, nor is it Rodin's, an attempt at always greater fidelity, at an essentially more precise exactitude ; it deviates, for his own purposes, along ways of his own. He speaks truth, but not without rhetoric.

To obtain grace, Rodin will say to you, you must begin with strength ; otherwise the work will become hard and dry. " Quelque chose de puissant," he will repeat, with half-closed eyes, the hands clutching upon the imagined clay. If you remind him of Baudelaire's saying : " L'énergie, c'est la grâce suprême," he will accept the words as the best definition of his own meaning.

The later manner of all great artists, in every division of art, obeys the same law of growth. Aiming always at the utmost precision of rendering his subject-matter, the artist comes gradually to take a different view of what precision really is. He begins by seeking a form which can express everything without leaving anything over ; he desires to draw his circle round some separate fragment of nature, and to exhibit the captured, complete thing. Only, nature rebels. Something remains

RODIN

Women Embracing—Sketch

over, stays outside the circle. The breath has gone out of the body, the mystery has gone out of the soul. He has cut off his fragment, if you will, but he has cut it off from life. At this point the public accepts his work; he seems to have attained. At this point he realizes how far he is from attainment, and he sets himself to the eternal search. He breaks down the strait limits of his form, he seeks to find new links by which to attach this creature of his hands to the universal life of things. He says frankly to the spectator of his toil : you must come and help me, or I can never tell you all that I have to say. He gives a twofold burden to the lines of his work : that which they express, and that which they suggest. The lines begin to whisper something to the soul, in a remote voice which you must listen in order to hear. The eyes have something more to do than to see. The mind must collaborate with the eyes, and both must be content to share with life itself the dissatisfaction of an inexplicable mystery left over at the end.

Rodin's earlier form seemed able to say everything which he had to say ; the modelling was infinitely detailed, the work lived with a vivid life of its own ; and what remained over ? Something remained over, the breath was not yet wholly lodged and at home in the body, the soul was not yet wholly conscious of its power of flight. He began to feel towards another form, apparently vaguer, essentially closer to the idea. He learnt how to indicate by a continually greater economy of means, by omission, by the simplification or synthesis of a great complexity of efforts ; he found out short cuts which would take him more swiftly to his end ; he built up his new form as much with the

brain as with the hand. The Balzac is a divination ;
everything is there, and it is there as it must be if it is
to be shown by sculpture : all depends on the sheer
science of the relief, on the geometry of the observed
profiles ; but the life, the mystery, the thing divined,
must be divined over again by everyone who looks at
it. The work is no longer a block cut sharply off from
nature ; it is a part of ourselves, to be understood only
as we understand one another.

III

IN one of Rodin's finest creations, a great hand, large,
strong, and smooth, holds in a paternal grasp a lump of
earth, out of which emerge two ephemerides, fragile,
pathetic creatures, with the delicate, insubstantial grace
of passing things, who cling to each other joyously,
accepting life on its terms of brief delight. It is God
bidding the earth increase and multiply ; it symbolizes
human life, in all its dependence on that unknown force
in the hollow of whose hand it lives and moves. Elsewhere he has indicated the vain struggles, the insane
desires, the insatiable longings, the murderous divisions, of the ephemerides, man and woman ; here he
indicates their not less pathetic content, the butterfly
accepting its hour.

All Rodin's work is founded on a conception of
force ; first, the force of the earth, then the two conflicting forces, man and woman ; with, always, behind
and beyond, the secret, unseizable, inexplicable force
of that mystery which surrounds the vital energy of
the earth itself, as it surrounds us in our existence on
the earth. Out of these forces he has chosen for the

most part the universal, vivifying force of sex. In man he represents the obvious energy of nature, thews and muscles, bones, strength of limb ; in woman, the exquisite strength of weakness, the subtler energy of the senses. They fight the eternal battle of sex, their embraces are a grapple of enemies, they seek each other that they may overcome each other. And the woman, softly, overcomes, to her own perdition. The man holds her in the hollow of his hand, as God holds both man and woman ; he could close his hand upon the fragile thing that nestles there, and crush it, but something paralyses his muscles in a tender inaction. The hand will never close over her, she will always have the slave's conquest.

Every figure that Rodin has created is in the act of striving towards something : a passion, an idea, a state of being, quiescence itself. His *Gates of Hell* are a headlong flight and falling, in which all the agonies of a place of torment, which is Baudelaire's rather than Dante's, swarm in actual movement. " Femmes damnées " lean upward and downward out of hollow caves and mountainous crags, they cling to the edge of the world, off which their feet slip, they embrace blindly over a precipice, they roll together into bottomless pits of descent. Arms wave in appeal, and clasp shuddering bodies in an extremity of despair. And all this sorrowful and tortured flesh is consumed with desire, with the hurrying fever of those who have only a short time in which to enjoy the fruits of desire. Their mouths open towards one another in an endless longing, all their muscles strain violently towards the embrace. They live only with a life of desire, and that obsession has carried them beyond the wholesome bounds of nature, into the violence of a perversity which is at times almost insane.

But always, in the clay itself, there is ecstasy. Often it is a perverse ecstasy ; at times, as in the Iris, as in the Muse who swoops like an eagle, as in the radiant figure with the sun in his hair who flings open the gates of the mountains in the monument to General Sarmiento, it is pure joy ; often, as in the Balzac, the Hugo, the Puvis de Chavannes, it is the ecstasy of creative thought. But always there is ecstasy.

In Rodin's sculpture, clay or marble, that something powerful of which he speaks has ended in a palpitating grace, as of living flesh. He feels, he translates, sensation for sensation, the voluptuous soft cool warmth of the flesh, the daintiness of the skeleton, indicated under its smooth covering ; all that is exquisite in the structure of bone and muscle, in the force of man and the suppleness of woman. The flesh seems to shiver, curdle, tightening upon the bone as if at a touch ; it lies abandoned, in a tender repose ; it grapples, flesh upon flesh, in all the agonies of all the embraces. His hand seems to press most caressingly about the shoulder-blades and the hollows of the loins. The delicate ridge and furrow of the backbone draw his hand to mould them into new shapes and motions of beauty. His hand follows the loins where they swell into ampler outlines : the back, from neck to croup, lies quivering, in all the beauty of life itself.

In the drawings, which constitute in themselves so interesting a development of his art, there is little of the delicacy of beauty. They are notes for the clay, " instantanés," and they note only movement, expression. They are done in two minutes, by a mere gallop of the hand over paper, with the eyes fixed on some unconscious pose of the model. And here, it would seem (if indeed accident did not enter so largely into the matter) that a point in sentiment has been reached in which the perverse idealism of Baudelaire has disappeared, and a simpler kind of cynicism takes its place. In these astonishing drawings from the nude we see woman carried to a further point of simplicity than even in Degas : woman the animal ; woman, in a strange sense, the idol. Not even the Japanese have simplified drawing to this illuminating scrawl of four lines, enclosing the whole mystery of the flesh. Each drawing indicates, as if in the rough block of stone, a single violent movement. Here a woman faces you, her legs thrown above her head ; here she faces you with her legs thrust out before her, the soles of the feet seen close and gigantic. She squats like a toad, she stretches herself like a cat, she stands rigid, she lies abandoned. Every movement of her body, violently agitated by the remembrance, or the expectation, or the act of desire, is seen at an expressive moment. She turns upon herself in a hundred attitudes, turning always upon the central pivot of the sex, which emphasizes itself with a fantastic and frightful monotony. The face is but just indicated, a face of wood, like a savage idol ; and the body has rarely any of that elegance, seductiveness, and shivering delicacy of life which we find in the marble. It is a machine in movement, a monstrous, devastating machine, working mechanically, and possessed by the one rage of the animal. Often two bodies interlace each other, flesh crushing upon flesh in all the exasperation of a futile possession ; and the energy of the embrace is indicated in the great hand that lies like a weight upon the shoulders. It is hideous, overpowering, and it has the beauty of all supreme energy.

And these drawings, with their violent simplicity of appeal, have the distinction of all abstract thought or form. Even in Degas there is a certain luxury, a possible low appeal, in those heavy and creased bodies bending in tubs and streaming a sponge over huddled shoulders. But here luxury becomes geometrical ; its axioms are demonstrated algebraically. It is the unknown X which sprawls, in this spawning entanglement of animal life, over the damped paper, between these pencil outlines, each done at a stroke, like a hard, sure stroke of the chisel.

For, it must be remembered, these are the drawings of a sculptor, notes for sculpture, and thus indicating form as the sculptor sees it, with more brevity, in simpler outline, than the painter. They speak another language than the drawings of the painter, searching, as they do, for the points that catch the light along a line, for the curves that indicate contour tangibly. In looking at the drawings of a painter, one sees colour ; here, in these shorthand notes of a sculptor, one's fingers seem actually to touch marble.

I V

RODIN will tell you that in his interpretation of life he is often a translator who does not understand the message which he hands on. At times it is a pure idea, an abstract conception, which he sets himself to express in clay ; something that he has thought, something that he has read : the creation of woman,

the legend of Psyche, the idea of prayer, of the love of
brother and sister, a line of Dante or of Baudelaire.
But more often he surrenders himself to the direct
guidance of life itself : a movement is made before
him, and from this movement he creates the idea of
the movement. Often a single figure takes form under
his hands, and he cannot understand what the figure
means : its lines seem to will something, and to ask
for the completion of their purpose. He puts it
aside, and one day, happening to see it as it lies among
other formless suggestions of form, it groups itself
with another fragment, itself hitherto unexplained ;
suddenly there is a composition, the idea has penetrated the clay, life has given birth to the soul. He
endeavours to represent life in all its mystery, not to
penetrate the mystery of life. He gives you a movement, an expression ; if it has come straight from life,
if it has kept the living contours, it must mean something and he is but your comrade in the search for
that meaning.

Yet he is never indifferent to that meaning ; he is
rarely content to leave any single figure wholly to the
chance of interpretation. Rodin is a thinker, as well
as a seer ; he has put the whole of his intelligence into
his work, not leaving any fragment of himself unused.
And so this world of his making becomes a world of
problems, of symbols, in which life offers itself to be
understood. Here is a face, fixed in an attitude of
meditation, and set aside unfinished, to which a hand,
lifted daintily to the temples, has found its way out of
another study ; and the man's hand waits, giving the
movement which completes the woman's head, until
the hand of the same model has been studied in that

position. Here two lovers, on the back of an eagle, are seen carried to the same point of heaven on the flight of the same desire. Christ agonizes in the Garden of Eden, or it may be Prometheus ; he is conquered, and a useless angel, who cannot help, but perhaps comes as an angel of glory, hovers down to him. A shoal of rapid Muses, hurrying to reach the poet, swim towards him as upon carrying waves. A great Muse, swooping like an eagle, hurls inspiration into the brain of the poet. Another figure of inspiration, an Iris, meant for the monument of Victor Hugo, is seen arrested in a moment of violent action, which tears the whole body almost in two. With one hand she grasps her foot, drawing the leg up tight against the body ; the other leg is flung out at a sharp angle, in a sudden, leaping curve. All the force of the muscles palpitates in this strenuous flesh ; the whole splendour of her sex, unveiled, palpitates to the air ; the messenger of the gods, bringing some divine message, pauses in flight, an embodied inspiration.

In a group meant for some shadowy corner of a park, among growing things, dear to Pan and the nymphs, a satyr grasps a woman with fierce tenderness, his gay animal face, sharpened with desire, the eyes oblique like the ears, appearing over her shoulder ; his hoofs clutch the ground ; one hand catches her by the hair, the other seizes her above the knee, as if to lift her in his arms ; she pushes him away, startled, resisting the brutality of instinct, inevitably at his mercy. Here are two figures : one, a woman, rigid as an idol, stands in all the peace of indifference ; the other, a man, tortured with desire, every muscle

236

RODIN
The Last One : Life—Sketch

strained to exasperation, writhes in all the ineffectual
energy of a force which can but feed upon itself. She
is there, before him, close to him, infinitely apart, and
he could crush but never seize her. In an exquisite
and wholly new rendering of the Temptation of St.
Antony, the saint lies prostrate, crouched against
the cross, which his lips kiss feverishly, as he closes
his pained eyes ; the shoulders seem to move in a
shuddering revolt from the burden which they bear
unwillingly ; he grovels in the dust like a toad, in his
horror of the life and beauty which have cast themselves away upon him. And the woman lies back
luxuriously, stretching her naked limbs across his
back, and twisting her delicate arms behind her head,
in a supple movement of perfectly happy abandon-
ment, breathing the air ; she has the innocence of
the flesh, the ignorance of the spirit, and she does not
even know what it is to tempt. She is without perversity ; the flesh, not the devil ; and so, perhaps,
the more perilous.

It is interesting to compare this version of a subject
which so many artists have treated, always in a spirit
of perversity or of grotesque horror, with all those
other versions, from Hieronymus van Bosch, with his
crawling and swooping abortions, in whom there
could lie no possible temptation, to Rops, with his
woman of enticing flesh spread out mockingly upon
the cross, from which she has cast off the divine body.
To Rodin it is the opposition of the two powers of the
world ; it is the conflict of the two rejections, the
two absolute masters of the human will. St. Antony
cannot understand the woman, the woman cannot
understand St. Antony. To her, he seems to be

playing at abnegation, for the game's sake, stupidly ; to him, she seems to be bringing all hell-fire in the hollow of her cool hands. They will never understand one another, and that will be the reason of the eternal conflict.

Here is the Balzac, with its royal air, shouldering the crowd apart, as it steps into the final solitude, and the triumph. It is the thinker of action, the visionary creator of worlds, standing there like a mountain that has become man. The pose is that of a rock against which all waves must dash themselves in vain. There is exultation, a kind of ferocity of enjoyment of life and of the making of life, in the great beaked head, the great jaws, the eagle's eyes under the crag of eyebrows. And the rock which suggests the man, the worker wrapped in the monastic habit of his dressing-gown, all supple force under the loose folds of moulded clay, stands there as if growing up out of the earth, planted for the rest of time. It is the proudest thing that has been made out of clay.

It is Balzac, but it is more than Balzac ; it is the genius and the work of Balzac ; it is the *Comédie Humaine*, it is Seraphita and Vautrin and Lucien and Valérie ; it is the energy of the artist and the solitude of the thinker and the abounding temperament of the man ; and it is the triumph of all this in one supreme incarnation, which seems to give new possibilities to sculpture.

V

JUDITH CLADEL, the daughter of one of the most original writers of our time, wrote two books. One is the life of her father, whose *Va-nu-Pieds* has always seemed to me not only a masterpiece in itself, but full of excitement, of fury, of imagination, of vehemence ; with an almost unique sense of pity where he evokes, in *L'Hercule*, the most grotesque tragedy I have ever read, touched with an unforgettable beauty.

Her other book is *Auguste Rodin pris sur la Vie*, at once a document and a living thing. The main interest lies in the exactitude with which it records the actual words of Rodin, much as he must have spoken them. There is a fine and subtle personal quality in the record, an inspiring and discriminating enthusiasm ; it is Rodin seen through a temperament, and the temperament of a woman who is also an artist. Nothing so valuable has yet been written about Rodin, because there is nothing which tells us so much about him in so nearly his own words, and with so sympathetic a filling up of the gaps which a man's own consciousness of himself leaves for the filling up of others. This book will have its value if it does no more than dispel the legend that Rodin was an *exalté*, following his own art by instinct, and knowing nothing outside it. It shows him, with perfect truth, as the master of his own mind, the philosopher of his own art, the profound artist incapable of saying anything of no matter what art without a kind of inevitable justice. In this book may be found the whole duty of the artist, not in the form of theory, but in a speech as simple as thought. When Rodin speaks, he puts everything that he has learnt into every sentence, as, in his art, he puts all his genius and all his science into every fragment of clay. Ask him a question, and he answers without pausing, like one who has meditated so long, so intently, and arrived at so certain a conclusion that the answer is ready, the question having been already asked and answered by himself. Of himself he speaks as if he spoke of others ; of others as if he spoke of himself. But it is above all of Nature that he speaks, of the unfathomable beauty of life ; and when he praises life it is like a priest who praises God. As Spinoza was drunk with divinity, so Rodin is drunk with the divinity of life. In the ardour with which he embraces and begets life out of life he is with Shakespeare and Balzac. And when he speaks, something of that intense yet equable flame seems to pass into one's veins, and the world lives with a more intimate vitality. " La Nature ! " we hear him saying in Mlle Cladel's book, " je suis l'admirer, maintenant, et je la trouve si parfaite que si le bon Dieu m'appelait pour me demander ce qu'il doit y corriger, je répondrais que tout est bien et qu'il ne faut toucher à rien."

There are few pages in this inspiring book on which there is not some phrase as simple and as final as that. Reading it with the sound of his voice hardly out of one's ears, it was as if one were still listening to him in that villa at Meudon, " presque vide comme un logis d'ouvrier, mais claire, saine et silencieuse," where I had so lately seen him moving to and fro in the midst of his white world of living clay. Some of the words are almost the same that I have heard him say, for, like every man who talks profoundly and sincerely about his own art, he repeats the same thoughts in the same words. And the words are often of that essence of literature which is rarely to be expressed in what is merely literature.

" Quand la voix des cloches est belle, on dirait que

c'est celle des arbres ! . . . L'art du moyen-âge,
c'est le monde en raccourci. . . . Ces femmes ravis-
santes ! (des pastel de Latour) on dirait des cerises, et
comme des cerises, on les mangerait. . . . Décidé-
ment, la lenteur est une beauté. . . . Une statue
brisée, c'est un chef-d'œuvre divisé en beaucoup de
chefs-d'œuvre. . . . L'artiste, comme la femme, a
son honneur à garder. . . . L'art n'est pas d'éviter
les défauts. C'est d'avoir une qualité qui emporte
tout."

How many and how subtle things are said with
" effortless energy " in just those sentences !

From the thinker to the artist, in Rodin, there is
not even a step. At Meudon, among many things
that I knew already by heart, I found one thing wholly
new, and, it seems to me, wholly new in sculpture.
It is a monument to Puvis de Chavannes, meant to be
set up in the open air, among trees (why not in the Parc
Monceau ?), and, as I saw it against the open door of
the studio, it seemed already to harmonize with the
green branches and the blue sky without. The composition of the group is by holes or gaps rather than
by masses, and its simplicity, like all fine simplicity,
is that of a geometrical problem which has come
suddenly to life. There is a plain oblong stone table,
on which rests, supported by a low and simple pedestal,
the bust of Puvis, but not quite as we know the bust.
The shoulders have been smoothed away, the features
as if a little veiled ; there is the same austerity, but
calmed, with less of the lean energy of the worker ;
and the head is as if crowned with a living crown, for
a slender apple-tree (to be cast in iron) rises from the
ground and leans over him, while a figure, resting one

hand lightly on the table and reaching out the other drowsily, is about to pluck an apple. It is the Bois Sacré of his own picture, an earthly paradise of some quite happy human joy; and this dreamy figure might be that of a peasant at home in Arcadia. The square lines and hollows of the table, flowing together in a single rhythm, the weaving of all this into one suave pattern, bring I know not what new enchantment into sculpture. It is not greater than the Balzac, but it is different, and not less a piece of living Nature. That was a rock, this is an orchard.

Near this monument I saw on the ground a great kneeling figure, which I recognized at once to be Ugolino in the Tower of Famine. But, as I looked, the man's likeness seemed to go out of it, and the likeness of a beast came into the hands, clutching the ground like paws, and into the neck lengthened and swollen into a beast's neck, and into the feline eyes, and into the mouth drawn open in a groan or growl which surges upward through the body. It is to represent Nebuchadnezzar eating grass, and the idea came into the figure, once Ugolino's, through some half-seen likeness to a beast, caught in passing, and developed in a series of conscious and significant changes. All Rodin is in this process, this way of letting well alone, this attentive observation of Nature. Imagination comes to him out of life itself, out of the physical form of things; so that he can say, as Judith Cladel has noted, " Je ne pénètre pas dans le monde des caractères ; je ne les comprend qu'à travers les analogies qu'ils ont avec les formes " ; form being to the sculptor, the passion, beauty, and meaning of life.